LEARNING, LEARNING

AND

STILL LEARNING

By Susie Mitchell Doswell

ISBN: 1-40332-460-3 (e-book)
ISBN: 1-40332-461-1 (Paperback)

This book is printed on acid free paper.

1stBooks — rev. 05/09/02

TABLE OF CONTENTS

FORWARD

I would like to recommend to you this book," Learning, Learning and Still Learning". I first read it while my sister was dying with cancer. It helped me at that time to help her and to be able to gain a panoramic view of life that I have been able to use in workshops, counseling and preaching. It chronicles one woman's painful journey to the peace which only can be found within. In this very poignant writing you will discover the faith which lays dormant inside of many of us which when exercised will empower us with strength to endure hardships and overcome obstacles. What does a person do when it appears that every time they recover from a trauma there is a new one awaiting them? What does a person do when they make choices that appear to be the best and then everything appears to turn out all wrong? Through this book you view a woman who has tried to pass life's test only to find new and often painful lessons waiting. It is her story and yet the story of everyone. This mother of seven shows the surprising twists and turns that life will give you and shares how each chapter of life is not about the test, but instead about the learning that perfects us and makes us great. These seven children are now adults who continue the legacy of learning. The story is the story of every parent, child and mother. It is the story of pain and victory. It is the story of life.

STANLEY J. HUBBARD
Minister, Jacksonville North Carolina

Dedication

TO

*Steven, Cynthia, Edward, Christopher,
Angela, Anedra, Alicia*

And

Wilson

THANK YOU!

ACKNOWLEDGMENTS

My sincere thanks to **STANLEY HUBBARD** for his editing, perusal and constructive criticism of this, my first writing attempt.

Thank you to my friend, **Shirley Ann** who insisted for years that I write this book.

INTRODUCTION

People, including my children have been telling me for years that I should write a book. At first we would laugh about it, they would say, "seriously", you should write a book. I agreed that maybe I would someday, when I could find the time and when I knew what to say. Time has brought me to this place in my life where I've said, I will write a book as God leads me to do so.

I have the desire to write to help my children understand their past. I want to write to guide my grandchildren in ways that I could not help their parents because I did not know what I know now. I want my mother to know and understand things that have been shared by others in my life.

I thank all of my friends who have been "true" friends to me down through the years, especially in the darkest times. They did not desert me. They always encouraged me with their love and faithfulness. YOU have been a real blessing to me. YOU know who you are!

I thank my children for their love and kindness. We grew up together. They refer to themselves as the "super seven" and they truly are super; each one in their unique and individual way.

I thank my mother and father without whom I would not have entered this life here on earth. I thank my only biological sister who has been a source of strength to me for many years. She truly is my big sister.

I thank my SPIRITUAL FAMILY, my mother in the Lord, who brought me to church as a little girl and introduced me to God. My life has been changed ever since. To my "special sister" and my other sisters, aunts, cousins, uncles, whatever, all of you who have touched my life for good. And of course, all of my many spiritual brothers who are ministers in the Lord.

I selected this title because of the many things I've learned and am continuing to learn. I am not an expert in any field. My training has come from my life's experiences and teaching from God's Holy Spirit.

When you've learned, you want to pass it on. It is too hard to try to tell everyone important to you what you have learned, so if at all possible that you can write it down, then you can get it to all who need or want to know.

I am sharing my life's experiences to add credence or credibility to some things that I have learned. These things are also principles or laws that govern this universe and everyone in it. They are not new things. I've only affirmed them in my own life.

I know that God gives life to us. I've learned that it is a school. In the process of our lives we are constantly learning as we go on this journey (life), to be the person, the real person, we were created to be.

We start as infants, totally dependent on our caregivers. We enter pre-school (whether naturally or formally) still dependent on our caregivers, then kindergarten, elementary, high school, maybe even college, less dependent on our caregivers. As we go through each of these phases in our lives, we also go through them in the learning processes of our minds. We learn independence, good and bad. There are good lessons, which correct and enhance. There are other things we learn that can misguide us on this journey. Our responsibility is to seek out and use the lessons we get at school (life) that are for our benefit.

I was a child with an adult voice. Though I loved to sing, I had no desire to sing all the time. I did not want a career singing, nor did I want to be famous. I have, however, always loved to learn and to teach, but I didn't think that was anything special. I have learned that it is special, especially if it is your gift. I know that it is one of my gifts because of my ability and capability to do it well and my strong desire in that area. If eel strongly about helping people to grow through knowledge.

I know that a person will change when they learn, if they want to be better.

I feel compelled to talk to and teach women and girls to be all that they were created to be. Girls grow up to be women and it is women who become mothers who have the power to shape and mold lives. It is very important that women know what they are doing before they become mothers. They have such power.

Although I have always wanted to go to college and receive a degree to prove what I know according to man's standards and to fully understand intellectually about life, I have not had that opportunity. I am thankful for the many things that I have learned through the experiences God has allowed to challenge my life.

ANCESTRY

It is so important to know where we come from in order to know who we are. We have characteristics, family traits that come from someone else. We are the sum total of a mother, father and their parents and their parents back as far as we can go in our ancestry or family tree.

Our thinking is shaped according to the way we were raised OR not raised. Even if there is very little verbal input from whoever raised us, still our thinking is shaped according to those genes within us, then the environment in which we were raised.

Each of us needs to examine our family tree and observe the strengths and weaknesses of the family. This is how to break negative cycles in our family; by learning what has happened in the past and why it happened. If we don't know what affects us negatively, we are bound to repeat certain behaviors over and over again through the family. By the same token, knowing the strengths of the family causes us to have pride (true pride) in ourselves that we can build upon and be strong, mentally healthy people.

This was one of the great harms slavery did to our people. The separating of us from our culture and our families. Many times children were taken from their parents and sold. Children were born outside of marriage to the masters or to those who were interested in mating strong slaves to work in the fields. The family unit was broken and for many generations to come, many of us did not know who we were. Neither did we know the importance of our roots or how it would help us to know and understand ourselves as individuals.

There were so many myths taught about us. That we were not people, but animals (with tails, even). We were treated like animals. If the people who owned our ancestors were to admit that we were people just like them, they might feel guilty about the treatment of our people. So they allowed themselves to believe that we were different in more ways than just the color of our skin.

At the end of slavery our ancestors were freed but many of them had no place to go. Most could not read or write. Though many of them were born in this country, this land was not their home. But they worked and helped build this country. They fought in its wars. They educated their children and did all they could to give them a better life than they had.

There was a time in our history when we thought we had to walk and talk just like white people before we began to discover our own roots—our own culture, and realize that we have always been a people since the beginning of time. The strength that it took to endure slavery in this country is proof of who we really are and who we were then.

FAMILY REUNION

I think, other than church, that the family reunion is the best gathering this side of Heaven. If you haven't known before, this is the place to go to find out who you are biologically in this life. Who your people were and where they came from. You can get a real sense of pride in knowing who you are.

Some people are afraid to acknowledge the bad things about their family. They think they're talking about them or betraying them. This is not so. Acknowledging family weaknesses helps us to not repeat the same behavior. That is, if you want to do better and be better. The family institution is God ordained. It gives us balance. It is our support system.

My family traces back eight generations and we've been having our reunions for twenty-one years. Our coming together every year has strengthened our family. We know that our family is African American and American Indian from the Black Foot tribe. We all came from Tennessee. I'm still trying to piece together as much of our history as the older members of the family know.

Each year our reunions get better and better and you can see how much it means to the younger people and the strength it provides for them—knowing who they are.

1

AS A CHILD

Fall is my favorite time of the year. Perhaps it's because that is when I was born, I don't know.

October 1941, I was born to sharecroppers in Memphis, Tennessee. They lived in the country in Rose Mark but came to the city for me to be born at the hospital Two years earlier my big sister had been born. She was born at home with a mid-wife and mother said she thought she was going to die, the birth was so long and so painful. She determined that if she had another baby, it would have to be born in the hospital. So I had the privilege of entering this life within a modern medical facility, John Gaston Hospital in Memphis, Tennessee.

My stay in Tennessee was brief. All of two months. In December 1941, my parents and we two girls left Tennessee and moved to Illinois. My parents like so many other sharecroppers in the south were leaving, moving up North for a better life.

Neither my parents nor their parents before them were educated folks. They didn't own any land. Some of our relatives did, but my parents did not want to farm. All most people could do was work hard for someone else. They heard that life was better in the north because you did not work as hard as you did in the fields chopping cotton and you got paid more for the work you did.

As sharecroppers, they lived on the boss's land and worked his crop. They charged whatever their needs were at the General Store and when the crop was brought in, the bill was figured up and whatever they owed was taken out of their wages. Needless to say, after paying the bill there was nothing left for you, so the process would start all over again. We had family members who ran away during the night and some that changed their names for fear that someone would come after them.

My father's father died when he was a boy. I believe he was about eight years old. He had one uncle and five aunts. They all doted on my father. They had all moved to Chicago, Illinois except for one aunt who remained in Tennessee. As a boy my father had the opportunity to go live in Chicago. One summer he returned to Tennessee and met my mother. He naturally drew attention since he had been up north, as well as, he was very good looking. My mother was also very attractive. They began to court, even though she was not old enough. They were married when she was fifteen and expecting a baby—my older sister.

In Chicago my father worked at the steel mill and my mother became a waitress. In 1939, my grandparents who were also sharecroppers had left Tennessee and moved to Danville, Illinois where my grandfather's brother had found plenty of work. My grandfather was a wallpaper hanger and my grandmother was a domestic worker and a cook. We were in Chicago and our grandparents were in Danville, 120 miles away.

I can remember as a child probably around three or four coming to Danville, Illinois to visit. Our great uncle had a car with running boards on the side and I remember coming and going back to Chicago in that car. I remember a few things about Chicago, which lets me, know that you can remember things that happened at a very early age. Our mother was stricken with rheumatoid arthritis and was bed ridden for about 6 months. I remember her lying in bed and my being hungry. I couldn't understand why she didn't get up and feed me. I remember crying because I was hungry. We had to wait until my great-aunt came home to feed us. After being grown for some time, I asked my mother about this memory and she told me abut her illness. My father was drafted into the Army during the war and we moved down to Danville to stay with our grandmother. My mother got a job and we moved into the little house next door to my grandparents which was also on their property. My father was only in the Army for ten months. When he got out, we remained in Danville. This is where I started school and where I was raised.

People always said we were cute little girls. They thought we were twins because our mother dressed us alike. We enjoyed having people guess which one of us was which. We loved to wear our hair in Shirley Temple curls. Our mother always cautioned us even as litter girls that we were not to think we were cute, that it was more important to be pretty on the inside. This was a lesson that I took to heart, which helped me to strive to not just be attractive on the outside, but inside as well.

People also always said I was "fast". I didn't know fully what that meant, but I knew it wasn't complimentary. It always hurt my feelings when I heard it because I knew I wasn't bad. After so many years of hearing this, however, I began to think maybe I was and I just didn't know it. They weren't talking about the fact that I was a fast learner, even though I was. I loved school and I loved to learn. I was an A & B student. I was encouraged to learn and to excel by my schoolteachers and my spiritual mother. We would have contests at church and I would always win for answering the most questions. My 5th grade teacher would always put mottoes on the board for us to memorize as motivation. I've always remembered from that time "success comes in cans, not can'ts. "I was active in extra curricular activities after school. I was in clubs and programs at school, at the neighborhood youth center, on the drill team, the junior legion, in choirs, etc.

My parents did not share in any of these things because of their work schedules, but I went on anyway. There was always some adult who would be responsible for me. My sister was not interested in the same things that I was so I was alone with others who had the same interests that I did.

I loved holidays because my parents would be off from work and we could be together. They were usually in a happy and festive mood (at least that's how it would start out). In the summertime we always went on picnics with other families that were my parents' friends. There would be a lot of people and kids; girls and boys. I was always a friendly smiling girl. And yes, I liked the boys. I didn't see anything significant about that because I liked people, all people. Boys paid me attention because I was cute and I liked the attention. Those were the happiest times for me because we were all together even though most of the time when we went home they would have an argument. Sometimes it would be in the car on the way home. My father would have had too much to drink and he would be driving too fast and my mother would try to get him to slow down. Then he would finally reveal to my mother what he was angry about and the day would be ruined for my mother. It disturbed us too but not as much since we were just kids at the time.

As I said earlier, my father was a good looking man and he had been spoiled by the attention my great aunts had always given him over the years. In loving him and trying to make up for his not having a father, they failed to make him be responsible. They made excuses for his behavior. Whenever he would get mad at my mother he would threaten to leave and go back to Chicago. We would cry and beg him not to go. He would bring his clothes back in the house until the next time. We finally wised up and stopped begging hin to stay, and he, of course, didn't leave.

My father was not a very good provider. My mother HAD to work even though there was only two of us children. He was a womanizer and a gambler so there was not much time for parenting or nurturing us girls, but we knew he loved us. Many a tine he would gamble away his whole paycheck. I learned to dislike gambling at an early age because of our suffering and my mother's anguish. My grandfather was a gambler too. He eventually lost the house that he and my grandmother had struggled to buy. None of this made sense to me. But I was a kid, what did I know?

The years brought much discord in our home. I was glad I was away from home a lot because I hated the fussing and fighting. The accusing, the different women calling the house for my dad. He was extremely jealous of my mother. She worked in the public and he was always accusing her of being too friendly with the customers. At first the arguments were not often but over tine they became more frequent until they seemed to be all the time. My mother would threaten to leave as soon as we were grown up. I began to wonder why she was waiting for us to be grown. I didn't understand why people would stay together if they made one another miserable. This was nothing against my father. We loved him dearly and we also loved our mother. We wanted them both to be happy. If not together, then apart.

Though things were not happy for me in my home life, all was not dark. Light had been brought into my life when I was very young. That light was from coming to know about God. Our neighbor also became my Mother in the Lord. She lived across the street from us. When the church of Christ was started in our neighborhood, she and her husband became charter members of the church. She went around to all the houses in the neighborhood and got the children to bring them to Sunday school. She was the organizer of all the programs and activities at the church.

So began my life in the Lord. I never missed Sunday school and loved hearing about Jesus and all the stories of heroes in the Bible. We had a junior club, which is the counterpart to today's youth groups. We met at her house at first. I was not a junior yet, I was a primary. She let me come anyway because she said that I knew just as much as the older girls. They didn't like that but I sure did. We learned many things that children need growing up. She really looked after us and guided our growth in the Lord. She was always standing up for us. When she heard of the Christian Service camp in our area she wanted us to have that experience of going to a camp like this. They had never thought about allowing "colored" children to come. (we were called colored people then). Of course, she challenged them on this. We were allowed to come and were the first "colored" children to attend Hanging Rock Christian Assembly in West Lebanon, Indiana.

I cherished those days because of my love for learning. We learned so much. This was a week of intensive study as well as fun activities. There were good teachers and I soaked it all up like a sponge. I sat at the feet of some of those who have become giants in our brotherhood.

I became a Christian and was baptized at the age of nine. I was so grateful that God would forgive me of everything I had done wrong and that he loved me. The fact that struck me the most was that he would never change, that he had been the same since the beginning of time and would continue to be.

My sister and I came forward the same day. We had not planned it or anything, we just both got up at the same time. We had to go to another church to get baptized because we did not have a baptismal pool in our church building. Though my mother did not attend church with us, she was there to see us get baptized. It was such a happy day!

The church family became my second family. Many times it seemed they were my only family. I was at all the services and activities. I could be depended on to do anything I was asked to do. I started teaching Sunday School when I was ten years old. I had sung my first solo when I was seven years old. I joined the choir when I was ten or eleven. My mother in the Lord was a lead singer. We had a great choir and people loved to hear us sing. When she moved away, I became the lead singer.

I grew up in segregated times. The church was segregated. There were white churches and we were the only "colored" church of our brotherhood in the county. Thankfully, we did not have segregated schools, but everything else in town was. We did have one colored school on the east-side of town. We lived on the North end of town so I always went to school with white children. Being the friendly child that I was, I also always had white friends.

My first experience with racism was when I was ten years old in the fifth grade of school. My friend, a Doctor's daughter was having a birthday party and she invited me. They had moved to town from some where else or perhaps she would not have been as friendly as she was to me, especially having professional parents. Anyway I went to their house. A black lady answered the door. She was surprised to see me. When she asked what I wanted I told her I was there for the party. She let me in. I remember feeling embarrassed because I did not have a gift for her. She and her mother assured me that it was alright. We had a good time. Then we were taken up North to a restaurant for sundaes. I had never had a sundae. I did not get to have one that day either. They refused to serve the group because I was in it . My friend's mother was so angry. We left the restaurant. Before that incident I didn't know that we couldn't go anywhere we wanted to in town to eat. I thought we went where we did because that's what we preferred. She then took us downtown to the movie theatre. Back then all black people sat upstairs. We loved to sit upstairs so it was no big thing for us kids. She was a smart and compassionate lady. So as not to repeat the incident at the restaurant, we all went upstairs to see the movie.

We experienced racism in many of the white churches we went to where people did not want to speak or shake our hands. We were only children but we knew rejection when we felt it. Since the county churches started our church, they supported us and would ask us to come and sing and have our preacher preach. So there was much interaction between us back then. They helped us when we grew to where we had to build another building for our worship. Segregation was accepted by everybody back then, until it was brought to our attention that it was wrong socially. Study of the scriptures further revealed that it was wrong morally in the eyes of God. We learned that as He created us all, He is no respecter of persons. God made us different on purpose. It was neither an accident nor a curse. Since God is no respecter of persons, Christians couldn't be either, and be right.

My mother in the Lord left Danville when I was twelve years old. She decided to go into full time Christian service and go to Louisville, Kentucky to attend Bible College there. This was a very dark time for us girls. Who would look out for us, who would teach us? There was no one else. It was a time in our lives when we really needed her, but she also had to answer the call of God that required her to leave us. During that time in our pre teens and teenage years, people would visit our church from the Bible Colleges to recruit students. At this time we could not attend white Bible Colleges, so we had two bible colleges who had been established for black people to go to. These were in Louisville, Kentucky and Winston Salem, North Carolina. I loved it when these people would come. When they challenged us about going to Bible College and becoming workers for the Lord, I knew that was what I wanted to do. But I was too young and I felt it was probably an impossible dream. But way back in the back of my mind, I hoped that one day I could.

Two and ½ years after my mother in the Lord left town; I became a teenage mother. I was 14 ½ when I gave birth to my eldest son. My parents worked at night and during the day. They didn't know who our friends were or what we were doing most of the time. Because of our upbringing, though, we were not out running the streets or getting into things that we shouldn't. Also we were raised at a time when all the neighbors looked out for the kids in the neighborhood. If anyone saw you doing anything they would tell on you. If an adult told on you, your parents believed them. Sometimes this was not fair but most of the time it was great to have the support of the neighborhood helping to raise the kids in it.

We lived about 45 miles from an Air Force Base. As we got older we heard stories about how airmen took advantage of women and that they were not to be trusted, that they were here today and gone tomorrow. I believed that but what I did not know was that there were boys in the Air Force, not just men. So as we went out to the teenage places, there would be boys right out of high school there who had joined the Air Force. Even some of our friends had joined and had been sent to California or Texas.

People from out of town always fascinated me because they seemed different. It seemed the boys from out of town were kinder and more considerate of you. The boys in town always said nasty things to let you know they wanted to have sex with you. I didn't like that about them so I usually to talked to boys from out of town. A lot of people came to Danville from surrounding towns for the social life there. There were a lot of places to go and things to do at that time.

I met a young man from Ohio. He was very quiet and not yet eighteen years old. He was usually alone. He rode over to town from the Air Force base with some older guys who dropped him off at the teenage spots while they went uptown since they were old enough to drink. I was a high school freshmen, cute and popular. We began talking and really liked one another. I saw him every—weekend from September to November. He told me one weekend that he was being shipped out. I was at that age that I just knew I was in love. I cried and cried. He was emotional too and did his best to comfort me. We embraced each other and wouldn't let go. He left at his appointed time. While he was at home in Ohio, he wrote me. I was sure that meant we were in love. He was sent to Texas where he wrote to me again. I went on with my life never expecting to either see him again nor hear from him after some time had passed.

I was shocked senseless when I realized that I was pregnant. How could this have happened? I was not a bad girl. I was not sleeping around like some were. I was so hurt and so scared and I did not know what to do. We did not have a talking relationship with our mother. In fact, we grew up in an era where we were told children were to be seen and not heard. There was no discussion between adults and children in our house. I told my sister of my predicament. She told her girlfriend who told her mother, who told my mother. I will never forget the pain in my mother's eyes or the disappointment I felt in myself. I did not know it was that easy to get pregnant. It was the night he left and we were standing up. I wished for someone to hug me and tell me everything would be alright again, but that didn't happen. I was taken to a doctor for a prenatal check-up and the doctor confirmed that I was pregnant. There were decisions that had to be made about the situation. I remember that abortion was considered but ruled out. It was also discussed if I would keep the baby. I knew my parents were disappointed, but not as disappointed as I was. I had interrupted my whole life, my schooling, my dreams. I had embarrassed my family, at home and at church. My burden felt so heavy. A burden I carried for many years because I did not know how to forgive myself. I repented of my sin and asked for God's forgiveness. I knew he forgave me but I couldn't let go of my guilt.

I have made so many mistakes out of ignorance. Not knowing what to do, then deciding on something that was not correct or the best thing to do. I did not know how to go to someone to ask him or her what to do and I didn't have anyone to ask. Many things I have stopped blaming myself for because I was a child and didn't know. From the time I had my son I was on my own and certainly not equipped at that age to make sound decisions.

7

I just kept compounding the trouble. One of the ways girls were dealt with who got pregnant out of wedlock was to be forced to marry the father. If she didn't get married she was certainly an outcast. There was a saying; "you made your bed hard, now you have to lie in it". I accepted this because I believed it. Even though we were not in the south, my upbringing came from parents raised in the south. I was just thankful that they did not make me get married. I did not want anyone to marry me just because I was pregnant.

I learned quickly that being ignorant about something does not do away with the consequences of wrong. My whole life changed as a result of this action. Though I didn't mean for this to happen, I had to live with these consequences.

My son was born a healthy, five pound boy. He was precious but I did not know what to do with him. I did know that I didn't want to give him away. I knew I could learn to take care of him. It helped that my big sister was there and she helped me take care of him. My mother continued to work, By this time she and my father were separated. He had moved out when I was fourteen and my sister sixteen. It was not popular or easy to get on welfare back then so it meant my mother would need to take care of us.

All the kids I knew were in school. Some of my friends were no longer allowed to have anything to do with me because I had a baby. I had a lot of time on my hands because the baby was asleep most of the time. I was not allowed to go back to school because there was no one to keep the baby. At this time it was rare when girls went back to school after having a baby. I knew one girl that had, I really wanted to, but I couldn't.

There was a boy that I had met back at the beginning of the summer the year I got pregnant who had returned to town to live with his aunt. He started to come over and visit me. He played with the baby and really seemed to like him. He became a regular visitor at our home. My mother was at work and I was glad to have company during the day because I was alone all the time. We became close and I felt that he really cared for me. I was glad to have someone care in spite of the fact that I had a baby.

I was fifteen and a half by now. What did I know about whether someone really cared. I didn't tell lies and I didn't think other people did either, at least not just for any reason. I was so naïve. I allowed him to be intimate with me. I didn't want to but I thought it was expected of me and that I really didn't have a choice.

You can guess what happened. I was pregnant again. I told him that I was pregnant and that we would have to get married. He said okay. So we told his aunt and my father since we both had to have someone sign for us to get a marriage license because we were underage. My mother and father had separated in 1956 before Steven was born. They signed for us and we

8

got married in March of 1957. I came home and told my mother that I was married and showed her the marriage certificate. I was fifteen and he was seventeen. My mother later told me she really cried that night. Being a mother now, I can really understand her pain and bewilderment. I had made a decision that was so unwise. I thought I was sparing her of having to take care of two children and me. I thought I should move out on my own. I thought I was fixing the situation for us. I was beginning to feel that maybe what people said about me was true. I lost all my self-esteem and thought I didn't deserve anything good.

I am including this in my section because it happened during my childhood. My next three children, Cynthia, Edward and Christopher were born from this union.

I learned no matter how bad things are, they can be worse. I know because they got worse. Eddie did not have a job so we had to move in with my mother and sister. Things were not comfortable. After a few months he took Steven and me to Western Kentucky to live with his father and stepmother. His father worked in a coal mine and he was going to get a job there too, or so he thought. I had never met such a mean man as his father was. He never smiled or had a kind word to say to anyone. He fussed and cussed at his wife all the time and sometimes he would beat her even though I was there. I felt so sorry for her. He totally ignored me and acted like we were not there.

Eddie deposited us at his father's house and left us there. He had another girlfriend there who he stayed with and who also had a child by him. I didn't know this until we moved there. His grandmother lived around the corner from his father and she was very kind to me. I could go around to her house and be away from the trouble for a little while. One day she told me that I needed to go back home to my mother. That there was no use staying down there to be mistreated. I agreed with her but I had no idea how to get back home. I cried myself to sleep many nights. I prayed and told God how sorry I was. I cried for my mother. One day his aunt came down to Kentucky to visit. She came in and said, "I'm taking you back home". I wanted to jump for joy. This was in July and I was in my eighth month of pregnancy. I said okay and returned back to Danville, back to my mother's, one month before Cindy was born. We had been married for five months. The marriage started out rough and didn't get any better.

By the time I gave birth to our daughter, my wayward husband had returned also. I was not happy to see him but I did believe that people were supposed to stay married. So he came and moved back in with us. Eddie was an angry young man whose parents had divorced when he was very young. He had quit school in his senior year even though he was very smart. He despised authority and didn't get along with most people. We were very different. As time went on it was apparent that this would not be the kind of marriage that I thought it would be. My lifeline was still the church. He had no interest in the church. He liked to drink and gamble, carouse with other women and shoot pool. He worked but he really didn't take care of us. I just went to church and back home. He became abusive, verbally and physically. He cussed at me all the time. He would come home angry about something that had happened and pick a fight with me. If I answered I was going to get hit or threatened. His aunt helped us get a little three room house so we could move out of my mother's house. I was pregnant again by February of 1958. I had never had anyone hit me before. I had never known anyone to get mad at you and you hadn't done anything to them. But this is how life was. I never knew what kind of mood he was going to be in when he came home. Even still, I was not going to leave him. I knew that I had gotten myself into this mess. I did, however, pray to God about it. I vowed that if he made a way for me to get out of this mess that I would never be disobedient again. I made that vow and I meant it. During this pregnancy is when Eddie beat me several times. I gave birth to my third child, Edward Jr. in November 1958.

I didn't leave but he eventually left us. He had many other females in his life and many other children that he fathered while we were married. I don't mean to put all the blame on him, it was a union that should have never been. Two KIDS who never should have gotten married. Though it was a marriage that should not have been I was sorry when it ended. I felt like a failure, that I had failed at something very important. The only thing in my life that made any sense at all was my life in Christ. I continued to go to church, sing in the choir, teach Sunday School and organized our youth group. I was only happy there.

Little by little, I let go of my disappointment. I became gainfully employed after the birth of my fourth child, Christopher. I was now eighteen years old. I acquired a house of our own and set up housekeeping. My grandmother stayed with us so that I could work. My grandmother and I became very close. From the time I had Steven, she would come to the house and visit with me. She told me that people make mistakes but they do not have to pay for them for the rest of their lives. I was very thankful to hear this. It helped some in my not thinking that I had to keep suffering for what I had done. I learned a lot from my grandmother about life in general. These were happy non-stressful times for me as I worked to make a living to take care of my family.

I learned from my childhood that grown people aren't always right. That all people in the church are not real Christians and some don't even desire to live what they talk. I saw their hypocrisy but didn't want to be like them. I thought that I wanted to spend my time helping teenagers to not make the mistakes I had made. I was now alone with four children to support.

While Eddie and I were married, in fact, the same month we got married (March 1957), I was involved in a car accident. I sang in the church choir and we were on our way to a small town in Indiana to sing one Monday evening, It had snowed that Sunday and there were a few slick spots but the men of the church felt the roads were clear enough to travel. We didn't have the entire choir, just two car loads of us. I was in the first car and my sister Louise in the second car. We were on a two lane highway and it was very dark. The driver of the car I was in was the elder of the church. He said it looked like something was in the road up ahead so he began to slow down. As we got closer he could see that it was a wreck. The cars were crossways the road. There was a ditch on one side with a car in it and a ditch on the other side. When he put on the brakes, he slid on a patch of ice in the road and slid into the wreck. My uncle was driving the second car. He slid on the same patch of ice and slid into the back of us The passenger in the back seat of our car was thrown out and pinned under the car. I was thrown underneath the dashboard in front and my head was cut open down to the skull. I was unconscious for awhile . When I came back to my senses I heard them saying that they had to get Jack from under the car. They literally lifted the car up and pulled him out and placed him in the back seat. My sister was calling my name. I raised up and told her I was all right . When she saw me, she screamed, "no you're not, your head is split wide open!" I raised my hand up to my head and sure enough, I felt the warm blood trickle down my face. They laid me down in the front seat and put my coat over me to keep me warm. I remembered my shoes had been knocked off and I was cold.

The ambulance arrived and put Jack and I into it and sped back to Danville. We held hands and tried to comfort one another. His legs were broken and he was in a lot of pain. When the ambulance would hit a bump he would scream with pain. I did not have pain because the nerves in my head had been cut. The ambulance attendants picked up one piece of my head and put it back with the other piece and taped it together until we could get to the hospital.

I remember my mother coming into the room, fear in her eyes and I said "I'm all right" smiling at her. I was so glad to see her. Then our elder from church came in. He was so distraught. He was grieved that anyone had gotten hurt. He had been taking us kids around for years and had never had an accident.

They couldn't give me anything to deaden the pain while they stitched it up because it was too close to my brain. So they sewed without anesthesia. I felt it and they said they could hear me screaming all the way down the hall. The next concern was the fact that I was three months pregnant and anemic. They feared I would lose the baby. I was hospitalized on complete bed rest for two weeks. I had several blood transfusions. My sister was in for two days for shock. Jack was in for a month. They put pens in his legs and he had to learn to walk again.

We were told by the elder of our church that we would have to sue his insurance company so that the bills would be paid. People talked about how much money I might get. I didn't know what they were talking about, so it didn't phase me.

The many church people who had heard me sing in different places really came to the hospital to see me and pray for me. I really looked bad at first. One of the white ministers who had helped to start our church came every day. You could tell the hospital personnel wondered who I was. My new husband came to see me one time only. I think he thought that the way I looked the night of the accident was the way I was going to look. One thing that I was sure of was that since I didn't die in the accident and I wasn't going to die, that there was something specific that I was supposed to do with my life.

As I said my mother and father were now divorced, but my father came to see about me. He went to see his lawyer for me and took care of the lawsuit. My mother never talked against my father while we were children and I always appreciated that. We could see for ourselves what his many shortcomings were. My sister and I continued to have a relationship with our father even though he married three more times after my mother. He helped raise those other wives children, doing more it seemed than he ever did for us. But we loved him as our father just the same.

Anyway, I think Eddie only hung around as long as he did because he thought I was going to get some money and he would get to spend it. He loved cars and thought he would get one with my money. But no money came. I met with the lawyer and he told me what would happen. I never expected that it would take years. Part of my treatment was that I would have plastic surgery for the scar that came down on my face. My hair would hide the scar in my head (which is still there to this day). I did what I was told and forgot about it.

I remembered the prayer that I had prayed about getting out of this mess I had made, but no money came until after I had delivered my fourth child in October 1959. I felt that this money was a gift from God. It meant I didn't have to depend on my mother anymore. Eddie and I separated for the last time when I was two months pregnant with Christopher. He was born in October and my money came in December. I got my full time job in January 1960. We were married and together off and on for three years. After getting the insurance money I was able to give my mother a gift to thank her for taking care of us and to furnish a house for me and the children.

Eddie came around trying to get us back. He threatened my life if he caught me on the way to work. I had a peace bond taken out on him. I was not afraid. I knew that death could not be worse than living like I had lived with him. I was determined not to go back again. I felt sure that I had been delivered. He finally left town and moved to Terre Haute, Indiana. He married four more times after me and fathered twenty one children in all. My children are the oldest except for the child he had before we were married.

Most of the girlfriends I had became pregnant also, just later than I did. (I was fast, remember). Most no longer came to church but I never did quit. It was the only thing that made sense to me. What God said, that I could read in the Bible and that had not changed.

I really was ahead of most kids my age. I associated with older girls and liked older boys. I started putting my age up because I looked older than I was. My body developed early which distressed me but there was nothing I could do about it. When I developed breasts my mother put camphorated oil on them in case they were swollen. But they never went down. I was also shapely and this made me a target for a lot of unwanted attention from boys since they would say the wrong things. I was ashamed that I attracted this kind of attention. It took me years into adulthood before I was not ashamed of my body.

Looking back, I'm sure it was good that I was stopped early in my years by becoming a mother. I did not want to be a bad girl, but I liked being hugged (not necessarily petted, but hugged). As far back as I can remember I had a boyfriend. It was innocent and I don't know how I knew what a boyfriend was except that it was a boy that I liked in particular. I didn't like all boys, there would be something significant that would make me like this one. As soon as I could write, I would write notes with his name and my name on it. I knew a lot of boys and I let them hug and kiss me, because I liked the way it felt. I did not like the boys that wanted to put their hands under my clothes. I know now that it was because there was no hugging or expressions of love in our home. I craved this kind of affection. I was a loving sensitive child who needed to receive love at home. We never "knew" we were loved.

I also later came to understand that I was easily made a fool of, because of this need for affection. If someone was kind to me, I thought they cared for me. It's taken me well into my adult years to discern what are people's true motives and actions, regardless of what they say. This has also taught me how to tell if someone really cared for me.

13

REFLECTIONS OF FEAR

Fear is a crippler that grips most people without them even knowing it. I have struggled with fear most of my life.

I believe some people are born fearful or full of fear because of their entrance into the world. For some people, it is because of their insecurities. Insecurities from childhood. If a child is not cuddled and loved (nurtured) from the time he or she is born, that child "feels" insecure. Some people learn about themselves, their insecurities, why they have them and how to overcome them. Some never do.

Fear rears it's head in may ways. It affects us negatively many times Insecurities that come from fear cause us to be afraid to look for a job, start anything new, find a house, start to school, whatever. Fear is within us because of not wanting to be rejected. Our first feeling of rejection came as a result of not having the nurturing we needed. That feeling of rejection is always there beneath the surface. We won't try new things or meet new people until we overcome the fear within ourselves.

I was afraid as a child from the time we were left alone at night while my mother went to work. This was way before I was ten years old. I depended on my sister to protect me. I was afraid of the dark, of bugs, noises and everything. She was probably afraid too, but she had to take care of me. We were always home alone at night. My mother worked at night and my father was gone. Eventually he worked at night too at his part time job.

I have endeavored to overcome my fears because it is a very uncomfortable feeling to be afraid of everything. I am an achiever at heart, so fear is uncomfortable because it gets in the way of accomplishments.

Someone wiser than me said to think of the worse thing that can happen, then accept that worse thing, then that will dispel the fear of that. This exercise helps in overcoming a particular thing but it doesn't totally dispel fear. Courage is not the absence of fear, but being able to function in spite of your fear. I have been courageous.

In the past I found that I did not want to ask anybody for anything because I did not want to be told no. I know now this was because of the fear of rejection. It is only a "feeling", not necessarily the reality. We try to be self sufficient so we don't take the chance of being rejected by anyone. The wounds of rejection from childhood need to healed. Learning to trust God first, to really believe that he loves and cares for us is what casts out fear. It is not a one time thing. Every time we are engulfed in fear, we must talk to God in prayer. Ask God for deliverance and deliverance will come. As you do this over and over, you can be freed from fear. Accomplishments bring a certain sense of security which dispels some fears. We must learn to add up all the positive things we have accomplished in the time we have been given.

2

INTO ADULTHOOD
(from 1957-1962)

The years I spent married for the first time were like a fog. Like someone put me on automatic pilot and I just lived from day to day doing whatever was necessary. I had a baby every year so that accounted for some of the fog. I knew nothing about birth control, plus it would happen so fast. There was no love making, just sex. When I was pregnant, he was gone. He would return after I'd have the baby. There would be sex, I would conceive and he would be gone again.

When he didn't leave, he would put us out. He'd tell me to leave, sometimes putting our clothes out on the porch. I would walk the children to my mother's house. We'd stay a few days, sometimes a week or two and he would come back and get us.

One time we lived next door to a gentle older lady who could see my plight. She didn't have much but she had a garden and fruit trees in her yard. She used to feed us many days. I would do things for her around the house or go to the store for her when she needed something. She would call me over and tell me she had cooked something and wanted us to eat with her. She always waited until Eddie was gone. I knew this was a blessing from God because we didn't always have anything to eat. His aunt would come by and bring a bag of potatoes and noodles or something like that. He would bring home a big box of whiting fish and expect that to do. I don't like that fish to this day.

I had cousins that would come over and play with the kids and help me with them. The girls from the church would come over too and play with the kids and baby-sit them if I needed them to. I would go to church on Sundays. Otherwise I was alone. My family did not come over. I only saw them when I was put out or when I came over to do my laundry.

One night Eddie was working on the T.V. and became angry when he couldn't fix it and began hollering and cussing at me. The kids were asleep and I was in the bed. He told me to get up and get out. I got up, got dressed and walked out the door. I was afraid of the dark streets and my mother lived about 2 ½-3 miles away. But I walked as if something was guiding me down the street. It was late at night, around midnight and I left the kids. I arrived at my mother's in somewhat of a catatonic state. She took me in and asked me where were the children. I told her what had happened. She got dressed and made me get in her car with her. She said we were going to get the kids. When we got there she got out and told me to stay in the car. I think she had finally had enough of seeing me treated this way. She used a few choice words on him, got the kids and put them in the car and brought us home with her.

I never went back to him again. I had three kids, one in my stomach and a stomach ulcer. I remained in a catatonic state for about two weeks. My grandmother nurtured me and I slowly came back to myself. When I came out of it, I knew I'd never go back again. Mother worked and supported all of us. My sister married and moved to Texas with her husband who was in the military. She was now expecting her first child. She came home for her baby to be born at the base hospital 45 miles away. This brought some happiness to my life. We were both expecting. We did things together like shopping and going to the movies. I began to smile again. She had her baby in August and mine was born in October.

One day my mother announced that she was going to re-marry. By this time I had received my insurance settlement. So she moved out and left the apartment to me and the kids and my grandmother.

I got my first real job the January after Chris was born. He was two months old and my grandmother was there to take care of him and the other children while I worked. I was now eighteen. This was the beginning of 1960.

I had a friend who worked in a Dry Cleaners and she was getting ready to quit. She had told me to come and apply for her job, so I did. The owner asked me if I could type. My sister, Louise, had taught me the keyboard when she was taking typing in school. She had a rented typewriter at home for practice. I told him I knew the keyboard. He told me to sit down and let him see what I could do. I typed my name and address and some other stuff. He said that was good enough, that he needed someone to type up daily reports, no speed was required, just accuracy.

I went home on cloud nine to tell my grandmother the news. This was again a miracle in my life. I had not finished high school. In fact, I was in the ninth grade when I had to quit. I was going to be in the front office, typing and waiting on customers. This was not common for a black girl. We didn't even have jobs in offices when we had finished high school, at that time, much less for someone who had not completed high school.

The man who owned the cleaners had a reputation, however, for giving black people a chance. He was supposedly part Cherokee himself. His head bookkeeper had been a black lady that we knew. She had worked there for years but was no longer there when I came. After about a year, I became the bookkeeper. I started at $30.00 per week, then $35.00 and then $1.00 per hour. I worked 42 hours a week and earned $42.00 which took care of all our needs.

The next years were happy for me. I had peace in my life. That spring we moved out of the apartment my mother had and into a five room house next door to our church. The house was large enough for grandmother to have her own large room and me and the kids the rest of the house.

Living next door to the church and with my grandmother being one of the older women of the church, we had the privilege and responsibility of giving hospitality to those who came from out of town to visit the church when there were more than could stay at our elder's house. Grandmother and I loved this. It was not a burden at all. We met such interesting people. My grandmother was an excellent cook and housekeeper and she could really show company southern hospitality. She was a good teacher and I learned well from her how to cook and keep a house. We would have long talks at night after I had put the children to bed. I loved those times of her imparting wisdom to me and telling me about her past and about life down south. She said I reminded her of herself in many ways.

While our new church building was being built, our house was used as a place of worship because we were next door and part of the church's property. We broke ground for the new building in November around Thanksgiving in 1960 and moved into the building the next Spring. Every Sunday, grandmother and I would move the furniture in the first two rooms and set up folding chairs. We had the piano and the pulpit and some folding chairs in her large room, then chairs in the living room. The other rooms in the house were used for classrooms and even the attic upstairs. We did that every Sunday for six months until the church building was ready.

My grandmother and I shared the same love for the Lord. She was a missionary minded woman who would help anyone in need. She had always wanted to be a nurse. Her gifts were teaching and taking care of the sick. Anyone could call her and ask her what to do when someone was sick and she could usually tell them. She always hated that she didn't get to finish school, but she was the oldest child and could only go to the seventh grade before having to work in the cotton fields. She never stopped learning on her own, however. Before she died, she was taking a correspondence course for nursing. She taught the teenage class at our church.

The Bible Colleges still came to the churches to recruit students. In 1961 when we were told that the President of the College of the Scriptures was coming and bringing a student with him, we were all happy. We had moved into our new church building and now we were having company. The president was to stay with our elder and the student was to stay with us.

To my surprise, the student was someone I had met in previous years. He had been a student in the 1950's when Mrs. Clark was a student as well as one of my friends from Champaign. In fact, his brother and I had remained friends down through the years. They were twin brothers from Texas; Herman and Thurman Jenkins.

We had a good time reminiscing and hearing about where everybody was and what they were doing. I found out that he had left school and joined the military. After the military, he had gone to Springfield, Ohio where his brother was preaching. He had lived there and worked selling insurance. After a couple of years he decided to return to the College to finish his education. He had been there for one year when we became reacquainted.

That was a special weekend. I had not had any male company in over two years and had not desired any. We found we had so much in common; our love for music, our love for the Lord and His church. We knew many of the same people. He was very intelligent. He sang for us that Sunday. He had a beautiful tenor voice. The weekend ended and he returned to Louisville, Kentucky. A few days later there was a letter in the mail from him. He was asking if he could come back and see me.

As an adult I had not had any male company. I had enjoyed his company and saw no reason why he shouldn't return. He said he would be bringing some other male students with him.

He came one Sunday afternoon and brought two other guys with him. One was a student from Pennsylvania and one was from Ohio. They were a hit with the girls at church. We talked for several hours, then they left. I sure felt special that he would drive all that way just to spend a few hours talking with me.

We continued to write one another. He expressed his interest in me. I couldn't believe it. I told him that I was not alone, that I had four children and I would never involve myself with anyone who could not love and accept them. He said that he knew that and he was still interested. We communicated from August to December when he came to visit for Christmas. My Christmas present from him was an engagement ring. It was beautiful! As we went to church on Christmas eve, everyone ooohed and aaahed over it. I thought to myself, is this going to be a miracle in my life? Was I going to be allowed another chance to be a wife, to have a husband who loved me? Everybody was happy and excited for me.

However, my bubble got busted when I got back home and he had left. My grandmother told me that it was not proper for me to wear an engagement ring because I was not legally divorced. I, of course had not given it any thought. Eddie had been gone for over two years. I knew that scripturally I could be divorced because of his unfaithfulness. I removed the ring. Thurman said he would help me obtain a divorce. He paid for half and I paid for the other half. I felt this really proved that he was sincere.

Even though I was looking forward to getting married, it was a dark day for me when I went to court. Eddie did not show up and did not contest the divorce. I didn't understand at the time why I felt so bad. (I came to understand it later). But most of all, I was grateful to God for giving me another chance.

MARRIAGE

I believe that marriage is one of the other great challenges in life, other than parenting.

Such a simple fact that marriage is a covenant between two people does not seem to be known by folks getting married. That two "different" people are coming together to become one unit. Marriage is God ordained. It was His idea. It is a divine institution. So, it should also be led and guided by God. It is not something to be entered into lightly, or by people who have not grown up (mature) yet.

In some cultures there are arranged marriages where the two parties have no say, just a contract or an agreement. Then there are the love marriages that have been since the beginning of time. Remember Jacob who worked for Rachel who he loved for seven years, got fooled by their father and got her sister Leah instead? He worked seven more years to obtain Rachel. It has been proven, however, that just two people loving one another is not enough or the divorce rate would not be as high as it is and there wouldn't be so many "troubled" marriages.

Our society, through movies and television, have instilled in our minds that love is magic. In two hours we see people meet, fall in love, get married, have a family and grow old together. We dream of that happening for us and to us. But this is make-believe.

One of the things that make marriage difficult is that both parties do not "hear" the same thing and therefore do not and cannot understand the same way. This is why communication is so important. One needs to know if they understand or even "hear" what the other person is saying. Most of the time we get swept away by the attraction and lose our reasoning capabilities, if we had any to begin with.

I firmly believe in real pre-marital counseling for ALL people wanting to get married. There is so much most people are not aware of about one another before they get married. Each other's baggage is brought into the marriage relationship. These are things such as unresolved anger from childhood experiences or other relationships, unrealistic expectations, feelings of insecurity and/or pain, or needing a parent rather than a partner.

The only reason two people should get married is that they met, were attracted to one another, got to know one another (which takes time), then decided to make a commitment to one another for life.

There are things you "must" know. First, do you even have the same values regarding what is important to you? Some of these are:

SPIRITUAL—your relationship with God. Do you both have one?

FINANCIAL—How you feel about money. Who is the breadwinner? Is this a shared responsibility? Who pays the bills and keeps up with the finances?

ROLES - How does each one see their particular role? As a husband, wife (what is expected)?

FINAL AUTHORITY—Where all disagreement can be settled.

PARENTING—Do you both want children? (this should be decided before marriage). How do you want to raise them? What values do you want to make sure they have?

One should know who they are and have even supported themselves on their own before entering into a partnership of marriage with another person. They should now what they have to offer and what the other person has to offer them. The union should complement both parties. They should both be better together.

Only after two people have gotten to know one another can they make a responsible decision to get married. They are saying they want to spend the rest of their lives with one another, have and raise children, or not, grow old together, etc. Not if it doesn't work, get out of it. It is your responsibility to do all the work necessary before making the commitment.

Needless to say, I knew none of these things when I married at 15 years of age, not the second time at 21 years of age, nor the third time at 35 years of age. I began to realize in my third marriage how much we needed to learn. I've not stopped learning even though I am well over ½ century old.

In searching my family's past, I've learned that we all knew how to get unmarried but didn't seem to know how to stay married. I decided that this too should stop with me and mine. I have diligently concentrated on learning how to be committed to the institution of marriage even if and when you can't be committed to a person because of lack of trust, lack of respect, or lack of communication. If you have something to work with you can have a peaceful relationship and a measure of happiness, while you work on the relationship aspect together. Remember how and why you got together in the first place and work from there. Difficulties can be worked out.

Marriage is work and should not be entered into without much thought and prayer.

3

MARRIED AGAIN

We were married in June of 1962. It was a private ceremony at the Justice of the Peace's office with my mother and sister as witnesses. One of my aunts baked us a cake and we had cake and ice cream at the house afterwards. Though this was my second legal marriage, I felt like it was the first time for me.

There had been no sex or lovemaking between us before we married and I was so proud of that. No matter how strong the temptation, we had endured and been victorious. It was very important to me as a Christian to be obedient in this way. Especially since I had messed up so bad before. I was striving to be obedient to the vow I had made.

We left Danville in August and moved to Louisville for him to finish his schooling. He had gotten a job at the Ford Motor Company to support us while he attended school at night. Going to school at night meant it would take him longer to finish but he was willing to do this. I went in the daytime with one class at night. Since I was a part time student, I also worked part time at the Day Care Center where the children were. This allowed me to be able to pay for their day care fees. I was thrilled to also have my dream come true. The dream of attending bible college. Again, I was taught by men who were giants in our brotherhood, such as: Dr. Isaiah Moore and others.

We had a nice three bedroom house in the suburbs of Louisville where the college was located. It had a fenced yard and plenty of room for the children to play. I was happier than I had ever dreamed I could be. All I ever wanted was to have a family and a husband and a house and be responsible and obey god. I thought I had arrived and I was so thankful.

Everyone was not happy for us or happy about our marriage which I didn't understand at the time.. They felt I was wrong to remarry and that he was wrong to marry me, because I was a divorced woman. We traveled with the college, singing and preaching in different places. Then we were assigned to a small country church over 100 miles away, one way. We traveled there every Sunday with our children and had services, then returned home. We left before dawn in the morning and arrived back home late at night.

We lived in Louisville for two years until my husband graduated with his degree in Theology and I finished high school and had two years of college courses. At the Bible College, the president got calls and letters constantly for preachers to come and start churches in areas all over the United States. So when he got calls from Texas and Pennsylvania, he asked us if we would be willing to go once we graduated. He came and talked to me because he said that he had learned how important it was to see that the wife is really in agreement when a couple makes a move, like this to avoid any discord in the home. Two years earlier, a couple had gone to Florida to start a church there and were doing good. They were older than we were and had been in the ministry longer. We talked it over and decided that we would rather go to Pennsylvania than Texas. We didn't know any one in either place.

RELATIONSHIPS

We begin our first relationships in our families. Here we are taught or not taught how to get along with other people.

My family, I believe had a healthy outlook on relationships with other people. It was on the golden rule principle. To treat other people the way you wanted to be treated. When we would do something wrong, we were always asked, "now would you want someone to do that to you?" The answer would always be "no". You would make amends and the incident would be over. We learned this behavior at home, school and church.

I was an adult and had been hurt in many relationships before I learned that this was not everyone's teaching or thinking. I found it hard to believe that someone would hurt you deliberately when you hadn't done anything to them.

It is true that if you want a friend, you have to be one. I have been friends to a lot of people who were not friends to me. I learned that friendship and even love is not automatically reciprocated.

People are usually looking for something when they enter a relationship with you. You should find out what that is. You should also examine what you are looking for in the relationship. If it doesn't provide what you want, the relationship should not continue., You don't continue a relationship for the other person's sake. It is a two way street, or it is not a healthy relationship.

Friendship carries the assumption of reciprocation. To say you are in a friendship relationship means you are a friend and you have a friend. A love relationship carries the assumption that two people are in love.

Most people want relationships. One should take the time to make sure the relationship is a real one. If it is not real, it is not worth the time, effort and emotion for a one sided relationship, for if it is one sided, it is not a relationship.

One should not try to use relationships to heal what's broken within themselves because it won't happen. If you were neglected, abused or mistreated as a child, you must seek healing for those wounds. If they are not healed, you perhaps will go into relationships with unrealistic expectations. In a marriage, many times, men want to be mothered because they were not properly nurtured, as well as, have a lover, companion and friend. Women want the love and protection they perhaps did not get from their father, as well as, have a lover, companion and friend.

Issues that need healing within ourselves must be dealt with individually because whatever happened, happened to us individually. The baggage or weight of it is ours alone.

Another person should not be expected to carry or bear the blunt of what has happened to you in your past. Sometimes when people say "why don't you grow up?" they are really saying, "why don't you handle your own stuff?"

4

OUR MOVE TO PITTSBURGH

My husband had gone to Pittsburgh, Pennsylvania to meet with the sponsors there and look over everything. Then he and I went up there for a youth rally where he spoke and we sang and met the people. That was the only chance we had to meet people and see the city we were moving to. This was a year before we moved. Then in June of 1964 we moved to Pittsburgh.

In 1963, while still in Louisville, we had a baby girl who we named Angela. I had gotten pregnant two months after we were married. I was not thrilled about having a baby so soon, but at least I was happily married so I took it in stride.

This meant that we had five children when we moved to Pittsburgh to start the church there. There was no nucleus of believers to greet us or be a part of the church. It was just us. We were to go daily and call on the homes in the neighborhood and ask people to let us come and study with them and invite them to come to the new church we were starting.

We located in the Homewood-Brushton area of the city. We had done a survey of the city before we moved and it had been determined that this was the best area in the city to start a new church. There were more home owners, thereby being less transitory than some of the other areas. It was determined that there were about 10,000 people in the area did not attend any church.. So we had a great number to draw from.

The first month we were there we had teams of people come to help us call and talk to people and pass out literature about the church and us. There would be a different team each week. The president and his wife stayed the entire month. Their daughter and son-in-law came from Ohio as well as our dear friends Jerry and Mary Alice King. Different churches brought our meals in for a month. Mrs. Norma Maxey, Roger Chambers and Jerry King are all deceased and never saw the church a reality in full.

When the month was over and everyone left, it was really a let down for me. There was no one to talk to without calling long distance. The impact of what we were engaged in really hit me. However, it did not change my mind. I meant that I would go anywhere I felt the Lord wanted me to go. I just didn't know how it would feel to be somewhere where you did not know anyone except your immediate family in the house with you.

Many people in the sister churches were very gracious to us. They brought food, offered to babysit so that I could go with my husband and volunteered to show us around. There was a director of the Evangelizing Association that was responsible for starting churches and paying our salary. So, we, of course got to know him and his wife well.

I had never lived in a city so large, had never lived where houses were so close together, had never seen that many black people in one location. My fears were dispelled only by feeling God meant for me to be there, so He would protect me.

The work was difficult. Coming from the Mid-West, and a predominantly White county, I felt like this was even a different culture. I had never been taught black history in school, and only knew about some of the traditionally famous black people in our past. It was very different to live in a black ghetto. This was one time when it was good to have a large family because at least we were not at church by ourselves. It did mean, however, that we had to do everything ourselves. We did have five or six people to start coming right way so we had at least 12-15 people on Sundays.

The association had started purchasing a two-story brick house in the neighborhood where we would live. We were to live upstairs and have the church meet downstairs. When they applied for zoning, the neighbors protested. They did not want a church in their block. They did not know who we were and had no desire to have a church in a house. Rather than go into the neighborhood with animosity, we decided to find someplace else to meet. We were to move into the house upstairs where there were seven rooms. When we arrived we found that the people occupying the house had not moved out yet. So we had to squeeze into the four rooms downstairs. They moved out within the month and we moved upstairs after we had painted and refurbished it some.

To get the association out of their deal we decided to purchase the house. They were to leave the down payment and we were to put the house in our names and make the payment from then on. This we did and rented out the downstairs apartment.

Thus began our life in Pittsburgh. Steven started the second grade, Cindy, the first grade and Edward and Christopher started kindergarten. Angie was the baby at hone, Ed and Chris were only 11 months apart, so they were in the same grade together until the seventh grade when Ed was skipped and passed to the eighth grade because his performance was so good.

We were what people thought was the ideal family. We were deeply in love and we were caring parents. We immediately got involved in the community. The neighborhood block club, the P.T.A., the Y.M.C.A. and places where we could help and get to be known. Thurman became president of the P.T.A. and eventually I was on the school's health board. We were as involved as we could be in the children's education.

Since there were no members to greet us on Sunday mornings, we did everything that needed to be done. The children helped with menial tasks and he and I did all the teaching. This was a missionary effort and I loved it, I felt God was using me to do something important, to start a brand new church in a neighborhood where there was not one of our doctrine. We built the church there. We had many experiences. We were in the ministry there for eleven years, or at least I was. My husband was there for ten years, I stayed a year longer.

We had a full church program of Sunday School, worship services and a youth group. We had many young people first and a few adults. We also had mid-week service and home bible studies. We had a full time babysitter so that I could accompany him to the home bible studies. Most of these were in single parent households where women had been divorced or never married. Most of my time and attention was devoted to building the church which took me away from the family a great deal.

We met many people, some who became members and were like an extended family to us. Many who we ministered to never became members. They had needs and we did our best to help fulfill them. Whether food or clothes, or a place to stay, finding a job or visiting in the hospital or at the jail, whatever the need was. Our phone rang day and night. This was a fact that my grandmother noticed when she came to stay with us for a month when I gave birth to our sixth child, Anedra, in 1966. There were the problem people as well. Those we couldn't help and those who had no sincere desire to be obedient to God. But that was to be expected.

During the time we were in Pittsburgh, my husband's twin brother moved to Detroit, Michigan to be the minister at the church where their mother attended. These were good times for all of us. Herman and his wife had the same amount of kids that we did. My mother-in-law was a Christian lady and very active in the church in Detroit. She and I got along very well. She had come to Danville to visit me and check me out before we got married. I did not take offense at this because I felt I could stand up under anyone's scrutiny. I had nothing to hide. She did not have the same kind of relationship with my sister-in-law, but that was between them. Whatever happened was before I knew them and I was never a part of whatever it was.

We formed a quartet between the four of us. My brother-in-law was a natural bass, his wife, an alto, my husband a tenor and I was the soprano. We were known as the Jenkins quartet. We sang all over the place, in Illinois, Indiana, Kentucky, Michigan, New York and Pennsylvania. We were good! We made dresses so we could perform looking good as well as sounding good. We really expected to go far, make a record album or whatever. We sang at the North American Christian Convention and the Eastern Christian Convention before thousands. We had a wonderfully talented musician who played the piano by ear, and lived in Louisville Kentucky.

In 1968 I met a family that also became an extended family for us. They were the Wilson's from Greensburg, Pennsylvania. Mrs. Wilson had become a member of an all white congregation in Greensburg and although she was happy there, she longed to meet others of her own race. While attending a North American Convention in Florida, she met my mother in the Lord, Mrs. Magnolia Clark. She asked where we were (black, Church of Christ/Christian Church people). She directed her to us since we were only thirty some miles away from her home. Upon arriving back home, she had her minister contact us to come and speak at her church. This we did. We met them and struck up an instant friendship that became a relationship that has lasted to this day.

Mrs. Wilson is a person that has been on fire for the Lord since I met her and before I met her. She immediately became interested in the work we were doing in Pittsburgh and wanted to be of any help she could be. This was a God send to us. We immediately put her to work as a Sunday school teacher. She also did evangelistic calling in the homes with us to set up home bible studies. She did not drive so it meant going to pick her up and taking her back home. Sometime we stayed overnight because we would be too tired to drive back home. We got to know and love all of her family. She became "Aunt Janet" to my children.

After traveling like this for some time, Mrs. Wilson decided that they should move to Pittsburgh where she could be of use every day. Her husband agreed to this. He got a job in Pittsburgh and they moved two doors down the street from us. She began working with the youth group. We formed a ladies group and a choir. We were thankful that the Lord was blessing our every effort in His name.

My friend that I mentioned earlier, Jerry King had died from a liver ailment in 1966 and left his widow Mary Alice and two children. I also had talked to her about coming to Pittsburgh to live. She and the children did come and moved into our downstairs apartment. Mary became the church secretary and one of the Sunday school teachers as well.

Mrs. Wilson left us in 1970 and moved to Louisville, Kentucky to attend Bible college and become a missionary. We had made it plain to her that she was not too old (she was 50). She has an extra measure of energy given to her by God. She went on to become an international worker for the Lord and continues to this day.

31

My mother-in-law came in 1971 when the seventh baby, Alicia, was born. (My grandmother died in 1969). She came and stayed with us for three weeks. She and I shared the same kind of stomach problems so we were always looking for a cure. She said she was going to see another doctor when she returned to Detroit. This was in June. In September she notified us that she had liver cancer. She died in early 1972.

The church in Pittsburgh was a training ground for many. We had summer interns from the Bible College. Many of our fellow ministers did revivals there. Many families used our home as a resting place when traveling to and from the east coast. We took young people to Christian Service Camp each year. We were also used in other places to carry on revivals and vacation bible schools or to sing and preach. Many friendships from this time are still mine to this day.

The children were growing up and being involved in school activities as well as church. Steven was interested in sports and played basketball and football and was on the safety patrol. Cindy was always involved in school projects as were Eddie and Christopher. They all sang in the church choir .I became glad that they were in a school environment that promoted pride in their race since I didn't have that growing up. Here, I too, began to appreciate who and what I was as a black person. It was also the time of the civil rights movement and the social injustices were very clear in this neighborhood.

We first rented a room in the YMCA when the church started, then we moved to an Eastern Star building. There we had classrooms and a large room for the worship service until we were able to purchase our own building. We bought a building that had been a Post Office and was on one of the main streets. We remodeled it and it became the permanent meeting place for the church.

All during this time the children helped in setting up the place for worship each week. Cleaning the building with us, putting out the books and bibles and whatever needed to be done.

I didn't know the pressures that the children were under. The pressures of being preacher's kids and feeling they had to "act" a certain way and couldn't really be themselves because certain things were expected of them.

Being a high energy person, I was involved in "the work". Looking back, even though I considered this to be the Lord's work, it was also my way of trying to be good enough to earn the Lord's favor. I needed to prove to Him that I could be good. I needed to prove to myself that I was okay. These were "feelings" in my sub-conscious that I was not aware of at the time.

In 1968 something else began happening in our home that I did not discover until 1971 when my world came crashing down.

PARENTING

I believe that parenting is the hardest challenge one faces other than marriage. It is on the job training. No one goes to school to learn how to parent, but perhaps we should.

You conceive and create a life. Then you are responsible for the care and nurturing of that life. No one else is responsible for the life you created. This is why parenting should only be undertaken by adults and not people who are still children themselves. One must first learn to be responsible for their own selves before they can or will be responsible for someone else, even their own flesh and blood.

It's a life long job. You are always needed by your children until you die. The needs change. In adulthood, it's just for reinforcement, encouragement, sometimes guidance. But you are always a parent and parenting is always needed. If you've been successful at it, you're needed to show someone else how.

Parenting has filled me with pride and joy. No one and nothing can fill you with pride and joy like your children. The love for your children is felt deep down in your soul; in the innermost part of you. No one else can bring such joy. By the same token, there is no such pain that can come that can cut as deeply as the pain from your children. Whether they inflict the pain or they themselves are in pain.

I used to be overtaken with grief about my parenting experiences. Such things as the fact that I did not have my children according to the Master's plan. I know that I made their lives harder than they had to be. The absence of a father is always detrimental in some way to a child's well being. The Master's plan was for each child to have two parents for their growth balance. Being a teenage parent, I, of course, did not know this. I was just committed to doing the best I could. I felt that if they grew up with anger, they would learn to be angry people. I didn't want that. I felt that if they grew up with men who were not moral, they wouldn't know and appreciate good morals. So, I felt that God and I could raise them if their fathers didn't want the responsibility. I believed that I could raise them by myself with god's help. We did raise them. God and I!

I have not regretted for one minute the way that they each turned out. I just know that they have had to struggle so hard for emotional stability and healing. This is what has caused much of my grief.

My desire is that my grandchildren learn about parenting before they become parents; that they realize the seriousness of the task.

I am proud of my children, the adults they have become. The successes they have achieved. They're responsible and moral. They take their parenting roles seriously and are good parents to their children.

My sister and I grew up without a father since he and my mother divorced when we were in our teens. and before the divorce, he was never there for us. I understand that feeling of incompleteness and abandonment. Even though our father was there in body, he did not nurture us and did very little parenting. The values we were raised with did come from both of them, however, and I'm thankful for those values that helped shape who I am. Most of my friends, male and female also come from broken homes. It is something that plagues our society. This perpetuates itself unless the cycle is broken.

It seems to be my quest and task to break these cycles that have plagued my life and those in my family before me. This fills me with a certain unrest. It is a positive unrest that motivates me to seek out and resolve what has been wrong. This is necessary in order for us not to continue to repeat the mistakes of our fore parents. I've learned that this is quite a process that is sometimes very painful. Looking back, digging down deep within one's self, seeking the truth, and passing that truth on to my children.

- ♦ I've learned that parenting is for responsible people who know who they are. People who have taken care of themselves (on their own). People who know what their values are.
- ♦ Parenting is for those who desire to have children. If, however, children come before they are planned for, responsible adults will know how to care for and nurture them.
- ♦ Children must be loved in order to grow and be emotionally whole.
- ♦ People who have not received love sometimes cannot give it.
- ♦ People who have not healed from emotional traumas received in their own childhood should wait and have children after they have sought help in dealing with their own issues.
- ♦ A parent must be truthful at all times.
- ♦ Children are loaned to us by God. We are to return them back to Him whole. They are not our possessions. They are not our trophies to be displayed to prove how wonderful we are. They should not be required to live our dreams, but must be allowed to

live their own dreams. They have a spirit that is uniquely theirs and must be connected to God's spirit for their well being. We, as parents, are to guide the process.

♦ Parents don't have all the answers and should have the wisdom to seek help anytime and every time there is difficulty beyond their realm of expertise and knowledge.

♦ The very best reward from parenting you can receive is when you see your children raising their children with the same morals and values that you raised them with.

5

TROUBLE IN PARADISE

As the children grew older I began to notice a change in Cindy which I thought was just puberty. She was so moody and her school work began to change. This was so unusual for her because she loved school. We were very close and I was proud of her. She was my first daughter. There were six years between her and Angela. She was my little helper and now was going into her teens.

I was concerned about her and began to keep an eye on her. Her teachers were concerned about her too. We couldn't put our finger on anything that was different to make her act like this. Finally, one day, one of the older ladies at church called me and asked me to come over to her house and not to bring my husband with me. I felt this was a strange request, but I did as I was asked.

She showed me some letters that Cindy had written her. They were love letters. I was mystified and shocked. She was old enough to be Cindy's grandmother and then some. I did not know how she knew these things about intimacy, nor why she would write them to a woman. I returned home in a stupor. I prayed and went into Cindy's room to talk with her. I asked her questions as to why she wrote the letters. She said she didn't know why. We talked for a while. I didn't scold or accuse. I just wanted to get to the bottom of what was going on. We were very close to this woman and her family but that still didn't explain this kind of letter.

I didn't sleep that night. I briefly talked to my husband. He had no answers for me. When I got up the next morning I looked in the yellow pages of the phone book to see if there was someone I could call. I called Children & Family Services and made an appointment for Cindy and I. I did not know what her problem was but I knew it was beyond my knowledge to handle. Plus, her emotional state seemed so fragile. This was late in 1969.

They began counseling with Cindy. They investigated our entire family. Everyone had to come in for interviews. They could find nothing wrong but decided to continue their observation with her. She went to meet with her counselor weekly which she seemed to enjoy. I think they felt she just needed some extra attention being in such a large family. They complimented our family and thought we were somewhat ideal. The fact that my husband was a stepfather who seemed to love the children and was involved in their upbringing was complimentary. Steven and Cindy's names had been changed legally when they entered school We all just went by the same last name. This was supposed to be just until we could afford the legal adoption of all four of the kids.

After a year and a half of this and many other letter writing episodes to older women, they did another set of psychological tests on Cindy that revealed that she was sexually active with someone. She was fourteen at the time. They called me in for questioning regarding our neighbors, other boys at the church, etc. I was completely stumped. I said she doesn't go anywhere alone. The children are always together. They leave home together and return together. It was one of our rules. Questioning her didn't reveal anything either.

I had begun to pray every since I knew there was a problem. I felt that we could deal with anything if we knew what it was. I begged the Lord to reveal to me what was wrong in our house. It was like a dark cloud hovering over me. Things had changed in our house. There wasn't the same peace and harmony. There were financial problems and the church was not growing and prospering anymore. There was much to pray about and I did.

One day I received a call from the counselor. She said Cindy had just left and needed to talk to me when she got home and that I should call her when we finished talking. We went in Cindy's room and closed the door to have our talk. I knew that this was the day that the truth would be revealed. I just felt it. I said, "I know you have been having sex with someone, are you ready to tell me about it?" She said, "yes", and then revealed to me that it was her dad, my husband. I tried not to show any emotion that would frighten her so I continued to ask her questions and she answered me everything I asked her. He had told her that she could never tell because it would kill me. It seemed we talked for hours, in fact, it was a couple of hours before I felt she had talked enough and I had heard enough. I knew she was telling the truth.

I left home to make the phone call to the counselor. She had sent me her home phone number. I had to get out of the house so that I could scream as loud as possible without being where I would upset her or the other children.

I called her and she asked me what I was going to do. I told her I didn't know what to do. She cautioned me that Cindy was very disturbed over the possibility that I would probably leave him and break up the family and the other children would be without their father. I still said I don't know what I'm going to do She insisted that Thurman and I come in to see her the next morning.

When he returned home that night from a board meeting, I confronted him with the news. I told him that I knew what he was so careful to keep from me. He tried to deny it but couldn't get the words straight. I had too many facts. Needless to say, there was not much sleep for us that night. I had so many questions, when, where, why, etc.? None of this made any sense.

I couldn't eat or sleep. I was seven months pregnant with Alicia. I kept myself in my room most of the time so the other children wouldn't see me crying.

The counselor didn't say anything about criminal charges or anything like that. She just wanted to help us keep the family together. This meant weekly counseling for us. He only went one time. Cindy and I went every week. I needed someone to talk to. I didn't tell anybody else because I did not know what was going to happen.

I was not allowed to leave her in the house with him alone anymore. The molestation took place at night while I was asleep or whenever I was out of town or when I was not at home. I suffered with the questions of how does this happen in what is supposed to be a good home. I wondered how I was to blame. I felt it had to somehow be my fault. I suffered over my little girl losing her innocence in this way. Her involvement with older women had become a problem. The piano player at church, the English teacher at school. The situation took over my life because there was always some fire to put out.

I had Alicia. Relations between my husband and myself were strained to say the least, but we were trying. The only thing that kept me was the scriptures that were in my heart about forgiveness. I knew I was being put to a tremendous test. How could I forgive this terrible thing he had done. The only answer I got was that I had to, that I had no choice. So I did my best. The days ahead were very dark.

Other incidents started happening that I was unprepared for. Cindy began running away from home. Though she didn't want to break up the family, she felt she couldn't stay. She left one day to go around the corner to the store and didn't come back. I was frantic and immediately called the police. Of course she had to be missing twenty-four hours before they would do anything. The twenty-four hours passed and she did not return. The police began to look for her and we looked as well. I walked the streets at night, crying hoping to see her somewhere. Even though it was dark and the streets were dangerous, I felt I had to do something. After a couple of weeks she was seen across the street at a lady's house. We called the police and they went over there and got her and brought her home.

It didn't end there. She ran away again and again. She threatened suicide. I sent her to Danville to stay with my mother for a while. She

38

stayed about one month. She came home to go to camp supposedly, and ran away again. She even went as far away as Philadelphia. I had her put in the hospital for emotionally disturbed children in a controlled environment where she could get counseling and to keep her from harming herself. She ran away from there. After a couple of years of this, I was worn out. I also realized that it was unfair to the other children to be spending all of my emotion on just one child. So I decided to stop forcing her to come back home. She was now sixteen and could quit school. She wanted to live with the woman she felt she loved and I could no longer fight her. We still had the responsibility of the church so I allowed her to come and get her clothes.

There were more incidents, more tragedies and more confusion. Cindy's friend's brother and two other men raped her at gunpoint one night. They took her out to a park on the pretense of needing directions somewhere and she was to show them the place they were looking for. After raping her they took her to the hospital and left her. The hospital called me and I immediately went to the emergency room. My feet could hardly carry me down the hall because I did not know what I was going to find. They had of course also called the police. There were two detectives there to take her story. She told them who had done this to her. She only knew the brother. After the examination she was taken to the police department to identify mug shots if she could. She identified both of the men who had prior criminal records. While at the hospital they asked if she had had sex with anyone else. She told them about her stepfather. They included this in their police report. They said it would be best for her protection if she was taken to the juvenile detention home until these men were caught.

She was there for two weeks before there was a hearing. The men were picked up but they had to decide what to do with her since she was listed as a runaway. They couldn't just put her in any facility because of her activities with women. I asked why she couldn't come home. They said she couldn't come home as long as my husband was in the home. I said, "well he can leave." The judge asked me if I could take care of it and I told him, "yes". I called my husband on the phone and told him what had happened in court. He said okay, he would leave. I told him we would come home after he had moved his things out of the house. We stayed at my girlfriend's house for two days until he moved.

The men were prosecuted and sentenced though it was a long arduous ordeal. As was normal back then, the victim was treated like the criminal. For months we went back and forth to court and told the story over and over again. There was no compassion from the system. There were very few advocates for victims of rape at that time.

We came home. I had the boys change the locks on the doors and we began our life without my husband in the house. A hard time, a sad time, but a necessary time. I felt that Cindy had been the innocent victim and she deserved any chance she could have to get all right. We surrounded her with love. I got her back in school. She got her high school diploma. But no matter what we did, it wasn't enough. Too much damage had been done. Far more than I knew.

My husband left our home and resigned from his position as minister of the church we had started. I was left with the responsibility of our seven children and the church. I had to face the leaders and the congregation and the community as well. But I felt the people were too precious for me to just walk out on them, so I stayed.

Cindy insisted on living her life with women in homosexual activity. She also had her share of physical female problems where I would have to take her to the doctor. She chose not to live with us and I only heard from her periodically. I did not try to force her to be in the family and did not know what to do about this choice she had made for her life, except to pray.

I fought depression on a regular basis. There were times when I didn't have the strength to get out of bed. I didn't understand what had happened or why it had happened. We had dedicated our lives to the church and helping other people to know God. There was no making sense out of what bad happened to us.

I had a wonderful friend who helped me in any way she could; she and her entire family. I struggled to feed us and keep a roof over our heads. My friend and her sister employed Ed and Chris in their businesses and Steven had a job as well at the grocery store. This helped to take care of their needs.

Though my parents were not together, they both felt that I should come back home to Illinois. I didn't agree. No one had been terribly supportive of me before so why would they be now, I thought. I didn't need any rejection at this time and space. I remained in Pittsburgh for another year, helping to run the church, securing speakers for Sundays, etc.

One day while wondering what on earth I was going to do, I felt something say "go home". I said, "what?" Again I heard "go home." I breathed what was a sigh of relief and said out loud, "okay." I didn't believe it myself. I even felt good about it. I called my mother and told her I wanted to come home. She said, "good, when are you coming?" I told her it would probably take me about two weeks to get everything taken care of, get a truck and pack up the house. She said we could store my furniture in her basement. This was one of the few times I could remember my parents being supportive of a decision I was making. That too, felt good.

I did not have money to move. I had no idea how it was going to happen, but I was sure it was what I was supposed to do. I told my girlfriend my decision. Although she did not want us to go, she agreed with my decision because she wanted things to be easier for me. I went to the church board and told them I thought it would be best for me and the children to go home and that I needed the money to do so. They agreed to give me the money I needed for a truck and one month's rent. My father and a family friend came up on the bus to drive the moving truck back for us and to help drive my car. We returned to Illinois in 1975.

It was years later before I remembered the many possessions we had left stored in the basement of that house. It had three floors. Though we had eleven years of equity in that house, we received nothing. We had a fifteen year mortgage, so the house would have been paid off in four more years. At first I thought I could stick it out until the house was paid for, but I couldn't. I was so glad to be leaving that nothing else mattered at the time. Someone benefited, I don't know who.

INCEST, MOLESTATION AND RAPE

I have always been outraged at these crimes. They are crimes committed on the helpless, against someone who can't defend themselves. I was appalled before it became a reality in my own life. Since that reality touched my immediate family, I have no tolerance for it at all.

It has been interesting to see the reaction of people on this subject, particularly men in my life who have been close to me, or men with whom I have come in contact. I feel that I have been able to tell where they are in their emotional control of their sexual desires according to their response in this area. I have seen outrage, anger and silence. Outrage and anger are understandable. Silence to me seems to denote some guilt somewhere. Either from their past where they have been victims of molestation or perpetrators; or, in the present where they have had wrong desires toward a child; female or male in their family or someone very close.

The reaction from women most of the time is outrage, hurt and disgust. Except in cases where women are in denial. Understandably, women would feel differently because of being in the position of the victim. In cases of incest or rape, they cannot or could not defend themselves.

Incest with children is so unfair. To take an innocent one's mind and tarnish it because of one's unholy desires or hangups with anger or sex is despicable. Children are gifts from God. They come into this world vulnerable to whatever and whoever they are entrusted. They are to be taught how to live life. They are to be loved and nurtured so they can grow healthy not just physically healthy but mentally healthy also.

MOST women that I have come in contact with have experienced either incest, rape or both. Someone in their family; father, stepfather, grandfather, step grandfather, uncle, cousin or brother TOOK liberties with them that they should not have.

I've even heard the dirty myth that it was the man's responsibility to "teach" the girl about sex, whether it was his daughter or some other female relative. This is a myth and a lie to allow a man to have his way with a child. And what is the explanation for damaging little boys? Men don't talk about the reasoning behind that! Let me assure you, there are no valid explanations. This is depravity at it's worse.

Man's desire for sex is his strongest desire, even before food. This is a desire that a man wrestles with all of his life, but is not a desire that cannot be controlled. It depends upon the individual's moral fiber, and his values. Pornography and masturbation heighten these desires, which is one of the reasons they should not be indulged in.

Because it is a crime that is done in secret and most of the time remains a secret, it gives a false sense of security to the perpetrators, causing them to believe that they can engage in such acts and never be found out.

Today, I am thankful that the covers are being pulled off of this sin/crime. I'm thankful that the government is taking the stand to protect women and children, especially children. I think it is a good law that requires sex offenders to be registered so that neighbors will know if a sex offender is living in their neighborhood.

I have children and family members who are survivors of incest and rape. I was molested as a child by an older cousin and the victim of date rape as a young adult. I have endured the pain of helping my own children recover from the perpetration of incest and rape.

Silence on this subject as on any subject allows people to hide with desires inside of them that need to be cleaned out and cured. Desires that are unholy and wrong. These desires can be overcome but only if they are acknowledged and admitted.

It is my intention to speak up and speak out on these matters because they are prevalent issues. They are issues among our society. They are issues in our churches. We should have no tolerance for this in our lives and this act should be numbered among all the other sexual indiscretions such as fornication and adultery.

If you force sex on anyone, it is rape. If you take sexual liberties with a minor who is a family member or have sex with a family member, it is incest. Sex with a minor is molestation.

This is not only a sin before God, it is also a crime, punishable by man's laws, which are based on and have their foundation in the laws of God.

6

COMING HOME

After being separated from my husband for over a year, taking care of the family and keeping the church going, I returned home in order to make our lives easier and be able to make ends meet.

We arrived safely in early January and parked the moving van in my mother's driveway. I told my sister that we would have a house of our own before the week was over. She asked how I knew because she didn't believe it was possible. I told her I had prayed about it and I just knew. I also knew we could not stay with my mother very long. Although she said we were welcome, I knew she wasn't used to having any kids around, much less, five of them. Steven and Cindy remained in Pittsburgh. Steven only had five months before he would graduate from high school and he wanted to remain and graduate with his class. Cindy was no longer living with us.

We arrived on Sunday and had a house by Wednesday. It needed painting so I made a deal with the landlord that we would do the painting for a break on the deposit and rent. The boys and I painted the whole house inside and moved the furniture in on Friday evening. The U-Haul company had allowed us rental of the truck until Friday. We settled in and were fairly comfortable to start our new life. The boys had a room of their own and the girls shared my room. We had a living room, dining room and kitchen also. I began looking for work the next week.

It felt good to be back at home because of the familiarity of it. It was good to see old friends and be back at our home church. However, I did feel displaced; having to start life all over again. I wasn't sure if I would stay at our home church or not. Things were pretty much the same as they were when I had left thirteen years before. I didn't feel like I wanted to give my whole self again to what was going on at church.

I began to go out with some of my old friends. I thought, I'm older now, I guess I'll see what's going on out in the world. My mother was in several social clubs and she invited us to their formal affairs. I attended and was the belle of the ball. It felt good seeing so many of these people whom I had not seen in years. But after the first one or two times, it wasn't what I really wanted to do. When I went uptown to where the clubs were, I ran into an old friend who asked me what I was doing in there. I said, "what do you mean?" He said, "don't you still go to church?" I said, "yes, so what." He said, "like I said, what are you doing in here?" I felt ashamed, but I didn't let him know it. I knew I had no business in there but I felt a certain rebelliousness against all that I had believed in. That was, however, the last time I went out to see what the world was doing.

My grandmother once told me that my paternal great grandmother (whom I'm named after) told her that the Lord's children have a mark on their foreheads and the world can tell when we don't belong among them. I guess that's what happened. It was clear that I didn't belong.

I decided to stay at my home church and get involved. We started working with the youth, formed a ladies group and a young adult choir.

I immediately looked for work and found it. I was hired in the federally funded C.E.T.A. program as an office worker. When a contract came through the office for an Assistant Auditor at our town's largest department store, they asked me if I wanted to go on the interview. I said "yes" because it could lead to a permanent job with more pay. I went on the interview and got the job. I knew God was smiling on me and I felt good about it. One of the benefits of working in the store was an automatic charge account if you wanted one, starting small at first. This helped me to dress the children and myself.

Though things were going okay materially, the emotional transition was difficult for all of us. I was back home but this had not been home for the kids. Even though I was back at my hone church, I was not looked on favorably by everyone. I was treated suspiciously by some and told what I could and could not do at the church.

My husband and I were known nationally in the church circles and through the bible college we attended. Our break up was devastating to a lot of people. I quickly learned that just because people are Christians does not mean they are automatically sympathetic to people who are hurting or in trouble. In fact, many times they decide that you must have done something wrong or this terrible trouble would not have happened to you.

Deep inside you wonder about that too, at times. You go over your actions over and over again. You are consoled only by the fact that you know you didn't consciously do anything and that God knows you inside and out.

The children and I went to many gatherings where we were sometimes snubbed, where people discussed me behind my back and made judgmental declarations, I later came to understand that a person who is a child molester doesn't have to have something present to cause them to act upon their feelings. It is a mental illness deficiency within that person. In our many talks, my husband assured me that I had nothing to do with his actions, that it wasn't because of some deficiency in our relationship. Needless to say, I still couldn't understand it at the time.

Having a house full of kids was probably my salvation. There was no time or energy for self pity. There was no one to depend on for my family's needs except me. I never did get any child support from the children's fathers, though I tried. The children began to adjust. We handled the conflicts as they arose.

I began to get some self-esteem back and enjoyed a certain freedom of not being a minister's wife. I could just be me without anybody's expectations.

The boys, Edward and Christopher decided they wanted to find their father and they wanted to wear their legal name of Matchem. I think they were seeking their own identities, as well as, expressing their disapproval of their stepfather and what had happened. They found their father living in Kentucky and working in the coal mine. Chris not only met him and got to know him, he found all of his half brothers and half sisters. He wanted to know them all. After talking with his father, his father told him that I was a good person and that if I had stayed with him, he probably would have killed me. I think this helped in their knowing that I didn't just leave their father for no reason but that I couldn't stay married to him. These moves made our family really seem mixed up, with the two oldest children legally named Jenkins, the middle two named Matchem and the last three named Jenkins.

Among the many friends we had in Pittsburgh, there was a family who rented our downstairs apartment from us. She was a divorced mother with three children. They rented from us for a few years before they moved out of the neighborhood. Her oldest son stayed in contact with our family. He had also become a member of the church. He went to the Navy and did a tour of duty. He still kept in touch and visited us each time he came home. When he got out and returned to Pittsburgh, we were in the midst of our trouble. He was very surprised but he was supportive of all of us. After my husband left, he was still supportive of the children and me. He checked on us regularly to see if we needed anything.

After I returned to Illinois, he continued to call me and even came to visit one holiday. He was a great comfort to me. He made no secret of his feelings toward me and the fact that he wanted to marry me. This was out of the question to me. He befriended himself to my mother, all of my friends and the people at church. When he got laid off from his job in Pittsburgh, he wanted to move to Danville, which he did. He got his own apartment, a job, and began to see me regularly. I was comfortable with him because I had known him for so many years and I knew he knew what had happened and I didn't have to explain anything to him. Other men had called me but I wasn't interested in starting any new relationships with anyone.

After two years, I finally agreed to marry Wilson. He had convinced me that he was a steady person. I knew he was my friend. I was not looking for a father for my children. I did not trust anyone for that. He was younger than I was (8 years) but I didn't think that mattered too much. I figured that I had really thought things through. It was not just about romance but friendship and companionship. I knew I wouldn't mistreat him and didn't feel he would mistreat me. Looking back, I'm sure fear also played a large part in my decision. I knew my children were not going to always be with me and I wanted to know that someone would be there. I just wanted to make sure that it was someone who really cared about me. The children were not happy about my decision to remarry anyone but I felt it was my decision since I knew they would be leaving one day soon and starting their own lives.

I was functioning everyday, taking care of everybody's needs. I thought I was just fine. I didn't know I was vulnerable and had not had enough time to heal from the traumatic break up of my previous marriage, or the fact that my marriage had ended because of irreparable damage that was done to our family, but not because we did not all still love one another.

It was ten years later when I lay sick in the hospital with stomach problems before I realized that I had never had any time to heal. I had never stopped. I had just added stress upon stress. I had become successful professionally and had proven myself in that area and was making good money. I had vowed that my present husband would not have to support my children so I worked diligently to take care of them.

I was not prepared for the judgments I received for remarrying. My logic and reasoning was that it would be better for me to marry someone to be faithful to than to sleep around whenever I became involved with someone, if I became involved. I was thirty-five years old, gainfully employed and not bad looking. People, however, were quoting the bible to me about remarriage as long as you have a living mate. I felt the marriage had been killed by the acts committed as well as a subsequent affair with someone else after he left. So I felt in my heart that I was not wrong. I did not have any counseling or therapy and looking back, I am sure I needed it.

I have since become convinced that divorce is wrong no matter what the reason. It is breaking a vow. It is not a wrong, however, for which one cannot be forgiven. I have begged forgiveness for my errors because of my lack of understanding of the whole matter. I am sure this will not keep me out of heaven as we understand it.

After I had been home for about four years, Mrs. Wilson talked to me about her desire for us to have a women's retreat. As missionaries we had many opportunities to attend retreats over the years but we were either guest speakers or the guest music. Of course, our women (black) were welcome to attend, but we were guests, not an actual part. We knew we had a need for our women to benefit and be a part of these kinds of gatherings. So she went ahead and made plans with the ladies in Louisville, KY to hold a retreat in their newly purchased church building. This was an overnight affair where we would sleep in the church building, have all our meals there and have workshops and share with everyone. I agreed to bring ladies from our church and the neighboring sister church in Champaign.

By the time this event came up, I had no desire to go at all. I had learned that my Angela was pregnant. My heart was broken for her and for me. I knew what this meant for both of us. I refused to allow her to get married, at least, until she finished school. She was a junior in high school. I felt the young man might some day resent her for interrupting his life and plans. I thought if they waited they might be a little more sure of one another and if they really wanted to make this step. At best, they were going to have some strikes against them. The young man was the son of a fellow minister friend of ours. They had not been going together. They just went out together while at a youth gathering. As parents, we supported them getting married, though they didn't agree with me making them wait. I felt like here we are again being held up to open shame for everyone to gossip. But I knew I was right to make her finish high school before getting married so she would at least have a high school education should she have to support herself.

They married when baby Jonathon was ten months old. We gave her a beautiful wedding (though she didn't wear white), and invited all our friends and families. Everyone came or sent gifts. The church was packed. It seemed our friends took this opportunity to show their love and support. Jonny joined the Marines so that he could support his family. He left for South Carolina for basic training. After he completed his basic training, he sent for Angela and Jonathon to join him. She left our home. This was not my plan for her life, but I wasn't asked. Angela had never caused me any problems growing up, so we were both very sorry about this turn of events, but we were willing to make the best of it.

Anyway, our retreat was a success. All of the sessions were so good that I couldn't stay in a down mood. The fellowship was rich. I had a chance to cry and release some of my pain. I came back home, ready to cope.

We decided at this retreat that we wanted to do the same thing the next year. We volunteered to have it at our church and I volunteered to coordinate the women in our area. This activity gave me a new lease on life. I began contacting people I knew in different churches and cities. They were interested and enthusiastic.

We planned and had our second retreat with over 100 ladies in attendance. I was so excited to be used in this way.

I received an invitation from the ladies group in Joliet, IL to come and speak at one of their gatherings. I was so surprised. I said, "do you mean me?" For so long I had felt like a fallen angel or something very different from everyone else. They said, "yes.they wanted me to come." As I made the two hour drive, I was filled with thanksgiving that I would again be speaking before a group of ladies away from home. I also was asked to speak in Cleveland, OH for their ladies group.

We continued the women's retreats and they became an annual event. It went from an overnight meeting to a weekend gathering of ladies from all over the United States.

After five years of these retreats, Mrs. Wilson became an international missionary, traveling outside of the United States. She asked me to keep the retreat going because it had proven to be successful. I had organized a structure for us after we had been meeting three years. We had continued to build on that foundation. This organization is now 20 years old. It is for girls from age 12 through seniors. We meet in a different city each year. We have a youth council of girls and advisors that plans the programming for the youth sessions. We have designed a Youth Debutante Program for those who want to give themselves to an intensive program of study and service. It is seven months long. They are then presented at the annual retreat.

After Angela moved to North Carolina, there were just the two girls left at home with Wilson and I. There was less strain on our family and more money since we both worked. As I said, I vowed he would not have to take care of another man's children, so I worked for those at home and to help those away from home whenever I could.

We were all active in church. The girls were active in school. We traveled a lot with the choir and to youth rallies and events in other cities. The boys were all married.

We were active outside of the home and we had a new undertaking in the home because of my remarriage. Wilson had never been married before and had raised no children. Visiting with us was great. Living with us, however, was a different matter. There was much to learn and to adjust to, as well as, much stress.

After we had been married for about five years, I felt sure we were not going to make it. I also felt that I was as dumb as a box of rocks in this marriage department. I have never learned, how to give up. It is not in my nature nor does it go along with my faith. He didn't want to leave me either. So, we began to learn how to be married to one another and stay married. Not just be married, but also have some happiness in the relationship. I've

49

seen a lot of people stay married because they felt it was the right thing to do, but they were miserable together. I did not want that kind of marriage. Twenty two years later, we are still committed to one another.

I've learned not to depend on anyone's approval. Like all children do, we want to please our parents, grandparents, relatives, etc. I did please then most of the time and I felt bad when I fell short. I wanted to be good to please others, then I wanted to be good to please God. It took a while for me to learn to want to please myself or to realize that I was as good as anyone else and to be happy with myself.

It always made me feel bad when people were envious of me. I guess because I didn't like anyone to dislike me. I've always had to face this. As a girl I faced it because the boys liked me and the girls didn't. People said things about me that were not true. The irony of this is that it continued into my adulthood, even with all the struggles and challenges that I seemed to constantly face. Coming home, broken hearted, constantly worrying about my daughter and her chosen life style which was against what I believed in, concerned about the other children's well being, I found that some people were still envious of me. This added to my distress. People assumed I was fine because I looked all right. Though I didn't go around inviting everyone to my pity party, my heart was broken. I learned over and over again how cruel and unfeeling people can be when the trouble is not theirs. There is a true saying about "church folks" and that is, "we shoot our wounded."

I have learned how to be confident in myself and that it is not a fault or my fault that God has blessed me with several gifts and the ability to exercise them well. All it really means is that more is required of me. I am an attractive woman physically because of my parents genes, not because of my own efforts, although I believe in doing the best you can with what you've got. I know how to love others without expecting anything in return. I am good only because God is good and I know Him and allow Him to be the Master of my life. Outside of Him, I am not good.

Many conflicts I have experienced working with people have been because of their envy and their not wanting me to receive credit for things I could do. People have had love-hate relationships with me. They loved me, respected me because of what I meant in their lives but they were envious of my abilities and capabilities. I have experienced this from men and women. I have learned to live with it. I know that it doesn't have anything to do with me. It is their own hang-ups that they have not overcome and if it were not me, it would be someone else.

THE "OTHER SURVIVOR" OF INCEST

The other survivor of incest is the other parent of the victim. You rarely hear about them. The focus is on the victim and rightfully so, and on the perpetrator. But there is another survivor-the innocent parent.

She or he is the one to pick up the pieces. They have been betrayed also. They feel hurt, guilt and sometimes even shame. They wonder what they could have done to prevent this tragedy in all of their lives.

Sometimes they are blamed by the victim. This is understandable too. The victim feels betrayed by the perpetrator, yes, but also by the parent who they feel allowed this to happen to them.

I know from first hand experience that it is not always possible to protect your child. I've heard of cases where children told and were not believed or where mothers knew what was going on and looked the other way or pretended they didn't know. This was not the case with me.

I did not know what was going on but I do remember when things changed in our family life. There was an unrest and a tenseness between my husband and my daughter that I could not understand. I questioned them both from time to time but they always denied that there was anything wrong. I prayed about it over and over because I could "feel" something was not right. I began to look at everything and anything that I thought looked suspicious.

My daughter was in a health class that was talking about sexually transmitted diseases (STD'S) and because she was having a discharge, she thought she might have one. She confided this to her counselor that she was seeing weekly. The counselor told her that she could not have this unless she was sexually active. So, she admitted the truth to her.

Perpetrators are usually clever and careful. They scare their victims into not telling.

I was sincere in my search to find out what was going on in my house and what was happening to my child who had changed from a talkative, happy girl into a moody person who wanted to be left alone a lot. My prayers were answered. Not because I discovered anything, although one night I almost did. He lied his way out of it, but I didn't believe him.

The encounters I was told were in the middle of the night when I was asleep or when I was gone away from home.

I learned of the sexual molestation of my son many years later when he was in college and began having seizures. He had repressed his childhood memories of his molestation from his stepfather, which began, when he was eight years old.

Just dealing with the initial pain, shock and anger over this kind of betrayal of trust is overwhelming. But, the other victim is the one to implement the healing process of the minor child while they are hurting badly and also need healing.

Most of the time when incidents like this happen, you are in no way prepared or equipped to go through this process. I found that there was little help available to me at that time. Certainly, no one was talking about such problems at church meetings. I went to counseling each week with my daughter just to get out of the house with her and try to find some help for us. My health and strength came from my prayers and the few friends of mine who knew what had happened and were just supportive of me.

We have waded through the many issues that come from sexual abuse, incest and molestation. We have worked through issues like the victims' mentality of low self-esteem, the blame game, the homosexual activity, drug and sexual addictions and the real pain that comes from this act.

We have also risen victorious only by the grace of God. Both of my children who were molested have been mental health counselors to troubled children and teenagers. My son is now an ordained Minister and my daughter is a Chemical Dependency Counselor at a hospital with her degree in psychology. They have used their past hurts to help others.

My healing has been slow but steady over the years because I have had to feel and endure their pain. Anytime there is an incident, I endure the pain again because I feel the suffering of those going through it. I can finally talk about it now, especially if and when it helps someone else.

7

MISSIONARY AGAIN

It has always been my heart's desire to work for the Lord. I was busy as I could be at my home church before I married my second husband. When he and I got married I knew that I could fulfill my heart's desire to serve God full-time in ministry. When our marriage ended I felt this part of my life was over also. But I was wrong. The invitations to come speak, sing or whatever let me know God still intended for me to be used in his service.

The invitation to help with the Women's Retreat and its subsequent organization under my coordination and direction made this fact clear to me. I was to serve differently but I was definitely still on His program. I sought His guidance in this undertaking and He gave it to me.

After I had been home for nine years we began to really search and see if we wanted to stay in Danville. Wilson was a Navy man and loved to travel. I loved to travel too so we began looking at places where we might move. I felt I had gained what I was supposed to by coming back home. Necessary healing had taken place. Things from my past—forgiveness issues from childhood neglect and abandonment. I was secure in my professional capabilities as well. My mother had come into our home church and was an active member which made us very happy.

The only stipulation we had was that it would be a place where we could have a church home and be of service. We considered a lot of places and became serious about moving to Lexington, Kentucky. Things did not fall into place as far as Wilson getting employment so we gave up on moving there.

We became acquainted with people from a church about 120 miles away in our capitol city of Springfield, Illinois. The Music Director there was interested in forming a mass choir of 60 voices between three churches within the 120 mile radius of Danville, Champaign and Springfield. As director of our young adult choir, I was interested. We all met together and decided to unite our three choirs. This immediately gave us over 45 voices. We traveled in Illinois, Indiana and Kentucky. We were very good.

This was a great opportunity to do something I really loved in the music area. I also was thankful for the opportunity to work with this man who I felt was such a talented musician. We became good friends and even discovered that our birthdays were just two days apart. We worked successfully with this choir for two years. He as the director and I was the assistant director. This was two years before we moved there.

During that time we also became involved with the church in Springfield. They were engaged in a large building program and from visual indications seemed to be a church on the move. Because of my experience in church work and in particular, church administration, I had a lot of questions and interest about their plans and how they would carry them out. We had become friends with the minister's daughter and her children then the minister, his wife and all of their family who were at the church. His daughter and son asked me about coming over there to help in the teaching area.

Little by little, we began to feel like we could be of some service to this church. It was a challenging opportunity. After talks and meetings, we started traveling over there every weekend to work with the young people and to train the minister's daughter and others to lead in this area of church work. We felt we had been of as much use as we could be at my home church. One of my first cousin's had been ordained into the ministry and had become the minister there. I felt he needed the freedom to grow and lead as he saw fit and not be hindered in any way by our presence.

The decision to start working over there was not made hastily. We prayed and weighed all the options we could see. I was really concerned about the travel realizing I was not as young as I used to be when I was doing this kind of thing. I really wanted to be sure it was the right thing to do.

We traveled over there every week for ten months until it got to be too much for me physically. We were coming home on Sunday nights, working all week and taking care of our family. Wilson suggested we move. Things were going well in the work and we didn't want to stop so we began making plans to move.

Having a missionary attitude, it was always felt that anything you gave up to do the Lord's work was all right. So we put our house up for sale and I terminated my good job. We were excited about working over there. I also knew that I could get a job there in my field and that we wouldn't be so far away from my mother. In looking for a place to move, I did not want to go as far away as I had been in Pittsburgh. I considered my mother's age and that she only had my sister and I.

We moved in the summer of 1984. We were there as missionaries for eleven years. We received no compensation from the church. We gave our time and talents and supported ourselves..

We were actively involved in many projects. We were also actively engaged in learning many lessons. The minister said he would like to see the church building in use every night. So I got busy to make that happen. I met with people in the community who brought in programs such as girl scouts and teen parenting into the church to go along with what was already going on. The youth group was thriving and we had a planned program to help in spiritual, mental and emotional growth. We hosted youth rallies and brought in many of our friends who were in ministry. We sponsored career days for the youth and other learning things from the community.

As soon as we settled in Springfield, my adult children started visiting. It seemed to disturb them that we had moved there. So, they came to check on us often. Maybe it was because we were there, the two girls and I and Wilson was still in Danville.

All of the guys lived in Louisville at this time. Angie and Jonny were stationed out west in Arizona. Cindy had joined the Army Reserves from Pittsburgh. After she finished she came to Danville to live for a brief stay but was now living in Milwaukee, Wisconsin. I only heard from her on holidays or when she was in trouble. I prayed for her safety a lot because of the crowd she was running in.

Things were changing in our lives. Angie had given birth to a little girl two years after Jonathon was born. Their marriage was eroding and they were both unhappy. She had come home to visit a few times. They were all home (except Cindy) for Anedra's graduation from high school just before we moved to Springfield.

After we had been in Springfield about four years, Angie and her husband split up and she and her two children moved back home with us. Anedra didn't know what she wanted to do after high school. She just knew she didn't want to go to college. Though very smart, she disliked school very much. I allowed her to take a break for six months but I told her she would have to go to school or go to work. She chose work, after two jobs, she decided to go to college. She enrolled in Robert Morris College and received a diploma as a Medical/Dental Assistant. This opened the door for her to become gainfully employed. Angela got a job and enrolled her children in school.

Wilson couldn't get a job right away so he traveled home on the weekends. During the week he stayed in Danville with my mother. This put a tremendous strain on our marriage and our home life.

Alicia was the only one left in school. She was very popular but she kept up her school work. Her friends were not ones that I would have chosen for her because they didn't seem to have any goals and their backgrounds were very different. She also was so loyal to them that she seemed bent on listening to them and not to me. When it was revealed to me that she was pregnant (a junior in high school) I just wanted to die. I sank into depression and wanted to just run away. Why? Why? Why? What was I doing or not doing that this would happen to us again. The same scenario. It wasn't someone she was going with. We had just come out of two years of a fatal attraction between her and a guy she was involved with. We were in fear for her life so many times. He had finally left her alone. Then this happened.

Emotionally, I was drained. One of my dear friends from Cleveland, Ohio came to see about me. I was serious about running away. I was just trying to figure it all out. I felt like no one was listening to me, no one cares what I think or feel, so why am I here?

Of course, I couldn't leave. I was definitely needed at this time. Who would take care of them if I didn't? I was still alone in Springfield with the two girls, Angie and her children because Wilson was still in Danville.

Some people were very supportive, especially the people on my job. Some others felt like I should not be teaching young people since I couldn't control my own? This hurt and shattered my confidence a great deal.

I took Alicia to my gynecologist who also specialized in teenage pregnancies and informed her that she would be having this baby. No abortion, but I would consider adoption. She said no to adoption. So, in March 1988, little Steven was born. She decided to name him after her big brother who had been a real support to her. We welcomed the baby into our home and our hearts. All the family came home, (even Cindy) to show their love and support and to encourage her.

After six weeks Alicia went back to school. She had a tutor in the interim. She felt so out of place at school after she returned that she opted to go and get her GED instead of marching with her class.

During this time, Angie and her husband divorced. He married someone from his hometown. She got her own place and a car and continued as a single parent.

Steven had moved back to Illinois and worked in two cities until he was laid off. His wife was from Louisville so she returned to finish her schooling. He moved in with Angela to look for work where we were. After some months of not being able to find anything in his field, he returned to Louisville. He had been a Law Enforcement officer for thirteen years but had left that for the private sector.

Edward had terminated his business dealings in Louisville and moved where we were too. He is a painter and contractor by trade and an excellent craftsman. He never went to school for this. It is his gift. He and his wife had agreed to separate. He got his own place and used our garage for his shop.

While Chris was between jobs, he came home but could only stay for a couple of weeks. He still had a lot of unresolved issues. So he went back to Kentucky to the things that were pulling him. He was no longer married but was the father of two children.

Cindy started communicating more. It had been 16 years since she had been really involved with the family. We began talking pretty regularly. Sometimes our conversations were heated. She was always the victim, always allowing someone to use her, always taking care of someone else. She always worked two jobs but never had anything to show for it, nothing for herself. I was constantly telling her that she was worth more than this. As we talked, our estrangement ended and she expressed her desire to come home and be with the family. We decided Christmas would be a good time. She flew home loaded down with gifts for everyone. It was like a family reunion. It was one of our worse snow storms. Everybody got stuck trying to get home but we had a marvelous time together. All I could think of was that you can never give up when you've prayed about something. We were separated for 16 years but I never stopped praying that she would come home.

After four and half years, my husband moved home to be with us. It was like starting all over again because we'd had to manage without him. Although he was home on the weekends, it was like he was visiting as the lord of the manor. The business of our living took place during the week, from day to day. I felt hurt, angry and like I had been abandoned again. I was allowed to make it the best way I could, especially emotionally. I had to be dependent on friends in the church if we had a need.

Life went on and we dealt with and learned from the many experiences and challenges we went through.

Angie became involved with a young man at church. In fact, he was the minister's nephew. Eventually they married. He had a daughter the same age as Angie's daughter Asia. Anedra dated off and on. At age 25 she got pregnant by someone she wasn't going with either but only seeing when he forced himself on her. When her son was ten months old they moved out to the east coast to Virginia Beach where she had a girlfriend who had left Danville. We helped her pack up her apartment and Wilson drove her and the baby out there. I'm sure she left because she was so disappointed with herself and she didn't want to be a burden to us. Alicia also became involved with one of the minister's nephews.. They were married before Steven was three years old.

I did a lot of self examination trying to see what I was doing or not doing. I came to the conclusion that I was too busy with other folks and had been for a long time. The work that I loved so dearly and felt that I was called to do had always taken me away from home. I had never given this any thought. I didn't neglect my duties at home so I thought I was doing okay. I don't know for sure that this is a factor that hurt my family, but I believe it did. The children not having both of their parents for nurturing coupled with my busy schedule did not help. It was not a requirement that I help run the churches where I was. I only felt I had to because no one else was doing what I could do. I also felt that I was working for the Lord and he would make everything all right in my life.

What was wrong with this thinking? It was only partially true. I've learned that you must always set priorities. If you've brought children into this world your obligation is to them first. This is doing God's will. To parent and nurture a child into adulthood is one of the most important jobs you can do. One must be sure that all is done that can be done for their children before they engage in something else outside of that responsibility. I don't mean be silly about your children, just be sure to see to all of their needs. Not just physically, but mentally, emotionally, and spiritually, know that their needs change with age and when you think they need you less is actually when they need you the most. They don't think so and will probably put up some resistance. But they don't know. Children always need their parents—they just don't know it. Parents should have enough confidence in themselves to stay in their children's lives until they are safely grown.

Anyway, as I decided that I had been too busy away from home, I began to make some changes. I let go of things that were really not my responsibility. I have continued to do this in my life. I decided that what God wanted from me was for me to be what I professed to be. All the work in the world wouldn't matter unless I was. I felt a peace in my soul over this decision, even though no one else understood what was going on or why I wasn't as available as I had been.

My grandmother had told me two things when I was a young adult that I was just beginning to understand. She scolded me one day about always being at the church. She said "Don't you know people use the church building to be doing things they shouldn't be doing?" I said, "no ma'am, I didn't." And I didn't know it then. That was not one of my experiences and I thought it was a terrible thing to say or even think. She also told me that people would use me if I let them and that they would use anybody who would let them.

You can imagine, since I was such a willing worker always the first to volunteer,that I was used a lot. Finally, at this time in my life I began to see that I always put myself in the position to be used. That was not my intent. I have always had a hard time thinking evil or bad of other people. I accepted them at face value and did not think anyone meant harm unless they showed that to me up front.

While living in Springfield, I learned about deceit and evil intentions at a level I had never imagined. These lessons have been good for me or I might still be very foolish as far as people are concerned. These lessons have helped me to better equip my children and others to realize how strong and how subtle evil can be.

I feel the eleven years spent in our capitol city were also for me to finish growing up. I was both useful and used. As a family we were able to look at the foundation we had and to build on it. This foundation stood scrutiny and testing. We have all been better for it. These were testing years for us all.

When I was fifty years old the "super seven" gave me a surprise birthday party. Angela did the planning. All the children and their spouses and the grandchildren were there. In attendance was my sister, her sons, my mother and also the surprise of my father. He traveled from Tennessee on the train. He was not well physically and he did not tell anyone he was coming. It was a great surprise all around.My father died eight months later It was the first time all of our immediate family had been together. This cemented and reinforced who we were as a family and how strong our ties and our love is. The children wanted to express their love for me and they did. It was a two day affair which lasted, Saturday and Sunday. They put an ad in the newspaper to appear on my birthday. They hired a photographer so that we could take a family picture and presented me with a framed picture of the entire group. This is a memory which we all hold dear and which said and did so much for me..

The last years we were in that city, we also engaged in the entrepreneurship of a restaurant that was not successful. I learned a lot from that too. More learning about people.

We resigned our missionary post after eleven years and after feeling that we had contributed all that we could in that location. We traveled for a few months encouraging the works in other cities and states. After 8 months we gave up our house and moved back closer to home, thirty miles away from my mother.

In my missionary work I have traveled all over the United States and outside of the United States to the Grand Cayman Islands where our friends, the Wilsons are. When we decided to come to where we are now it was because we felt we could be of service to this small congregation.

Each time we've moved or made a change I've thought it was for the last time. I say, after all, I'm getting too old to be moving and moving. But at the same time we affirm that we are willing to be vessels for God's use and his glory wherever he sees fit to use us. As with all the places where we have had the opportunity to serve, we have built lasting friendships and have fond memories and lasting lessons..

WHOLENESS OR WELLNESS

Jesus' miracles where he healed the body, then told the person to go and sin no more indicates that our wholeness or lack thereof is because of sin. Sin we committed? Not necessarily so. But sin, which is transgression from God's laws. And, from the beginning of time, sin is paid for in consequences. Cause and effect or reaping what is sown. Maybe it is your sin, maybe sin that you had nothing to do with except, reap the consequences. Never the less, sin was the initiator.

In order to be made whole, we must search and see what is broken and how it got broken. God is the master repairman. He will and can only repair what <u>you know</u> is broken and you take to him to be repaired.

We are all wounded in childhood. Whether those wounds are healed depends on whether we have had proper nurturing (parenting). Whether from biological parents, grandparents, guardians, whoever. One of the parenting roles is helping to heal wounds sustained during childhood. If and when that is not fulfilled we go into adulthood wounded, feeling rejection and fear and seeking healing most of the time in our relationships with others. We usually are not aware of this.

If you came from a broken home, you have some automatic issues of being deprived of one of your parents. If you were abused, you have some automatic issues of betrayal and distrust. These issues are in your soul (spirit).

Since sin is in every person because it is a human condition, then every person is sin sick and has the need for healing or wholeness in our souls. We go to the doctor for our bodies but not our souls. Many times if healing was done to the soul, there would be no physical malady.

The soul is where the heart (mind) is. "As a man thinketh in his heart, so is he", the bible says. The soul needs to be healthy so the entire person can be healthy. The soul resides in this house or tent called the body. We must treat the soul for wellness as well as the body. This kind of healing comes from God when we realize that we are more than flesh and blood with cares and desires.

I am convinced that one of the fruits on God's "healing tree" is knowledge. Knowing the truth is what sets us free; even our souls. We must be learning in order to heal or be made whole. We need to be learning who we are and what is broken about us and why. Then, most importantly, learning who God is, making the connection between His spirit and our spirit.

The songwriter says, "there is a balm (salve) in Gilead, to make the wounded whole, there is a balm in Gilead, to save the sin sick soul.

Our lack of wellness in our souls manifests itself in many ways. Some of which are overeating, alcohol and drug addictions, broken relationships, fear, depression, stress, poor health, etc.

When we learn something, we don't always put it into practice right away because it doesn't always reach us emotionally. It just goes into our intellect. But, if we never learn, there is no possibility for healing or change.

"You shall know the truth and the truth shall set you free." We must accept the truth about ourselves, whatever that truth is before we will accept the healing for our soul (spirit). We are both weak and strong, good and bad, fair and unfair. God knows all about us and loves us just as we are. We must love ourselves, also, admitting who we are.

8

THE SURPRISE CONCLUSION

While the children were growing up and during the happy times, we all wore the same family name of Jenkins. I never made a secret of our past, Steven being born out of wedlock or the three children from my first marriage. When I married the second time, our intentions, were that the first four children would be adopted and we would all have the same name. When we investigated all the procedures, we were not able financially to do this at the time. We decided to go ahead and just change the two older names legally because they were starting school and we planned to complete everything later.

As the children grew older, Steven was bothered about wanting to know his real father. After he became an adult he was bothered with bouts of depression and anger. I would feel so hurt and guilty. Finally, I realized that the only thing I could do was to try to one day locate his father or help him to locate him.

I contacted my friends in Cleveland and solicited their help. I gave them all the information I knew. We always came to a dead end.

I gave Steven all the information I could remember. When he moved back to central Illinois, I suggested he go to the Air Force Base to see if we could come up with anything, but he never did.

One day when Chris and I were talking, I told him how much I would like to find Steven's father. He said Steven had also mentioned it to him. They began to search the internet. Whenever Steven got information that he thought would be helpful, he would send it to me. I would send it to my friends in Cleveland. I decided it would be good if I could do this by his 40th birthday, but nothing happened by then.

Christopher got an urge one day and started the search again around April, 1998. He came up with a name and address in Akron, Ohio. We agreed that he would write a letter to that address. We allowed several weeks but no answer came. He decided to call the number listed to see if the letter was received and if this was who we were looking for. A woman answered and acknowledged receipt of the letter and said she was the ex-wife of Leon, Steven's father. She said he had moved back to Cleveland but wouldn't give any more information.

Further search on the internet gave us several names in Cleveland. Chris called me and asked if I knew his birthdate. I gave it to him and he said that there was a number that he was going to try. He called me back, so excited. He had called the number and got the answering machine. He said that the man's voice sounded so much like Steven that he was sure this was the right person. He said he left a message that told him who he was and why he was looking for him. He had some dates wrong so I gave him the correct dates of when he was at the Air Force base. He decided to call back. This time, Leon answered the phone himself. He asked Chris what was this about and why was he looking for him Chris reiterated that Steven just wanted to know who he was and to get to meet him. He admitted that he was who we were looking for. He was pleasant and gave Chris permission to give this information to Steven. This was June, 1998, one month before Steven was 41.

Chris called Steven and gave him the news. Steven was overcome and began to weep as well as express his heartfelt thanks. When Chris called me, I asked for the number also. I felt I just had to call. I had not had any communication with this person for 41 years! I was excited and nervous, but I had to call.

When he answered, I told him it was me and how bad Steven wanted to meet him. I explained that he didn't want anything from him except to know who he is. He told me that he was sorry for not trying to reach me way back then but that after a while he had forgotten what my last name was. I told him I didn't blame him or hold anything against him because we were both kids at the time.

We exchanged pleasantries and I hung up, totally shook up and elated over this turn of events. I then called Steven and we shared our joy. He said he was going to call that evening.

He called and they talked. Steven decided to go to Cleveland to meet him over the 4th of July holiday.

To our delight, the meeting was great. Steven stayed with his father at his apartment and met his half brother who is also named Steven, and his family. He met his paternal grandmother and her husband. He came back home, joyful and satisfied. He said it was like looking in a mirror and that he understood himself so much better. He and his father liked the same things and he has many characteristics like him. They were all pleased with him too. His grandmother said she wanted to meet me, that she wanted to meet the woman who had raised a son like him.

I called Leon after their meeting to see how he felt. He thanked me and complimented me. I knew I had to be in Cleveland for a meeting so I told him I would call him when I was in town.

I went to Cleveland in September for my meeting and I called him as I promised I would. He came and picked me up and took me to lunch. We began to get reacquainted. I took pictures of me as a girl when he knew me.

It was a pleasant time and we shared delight over how our son had turned out, especially with me having been so young when he was born.

Then he took me to meet his parents. They welcomed me with open arms of love. We talked and talked like old friends. They, of course, marveled at our finding Leon after all these years.

We went out sightseeing and to dinner and continued our getting to know one another. We parted with all of us vowing to never again lose touch with one another.

I went back to my hotel on cloud-9 knowing that God was smiling down on me once again.

I would have to write many books to tell of all the experiences and challenges that my children and I have faced. I would have to write books to tell about each one of them individually. I have written just a little to impart knowledge and give hope.

No matter what choices you have made and no matter how bad they are, you can always begin again. A bad experience does not have to mean the end. The arms of God are always open to all of us to return to Him and begin again.

I wouldn't trade my journey with anyone else, for I am still learning.

THANK YOU LORD!!

ABUSE

My definition of abuse is that it is the misuse of power, physical, mental or verbal over someone else. Regardless of how a person comes by the power, misuse of it is abuse. When you intentionally mistreat someone in any way, that is abuse.

My father was abusive. He mistreated my mother over and over again by his unfaithfulness, his lack of responsibility to take care of and provide for us, his physical and verbal negative actions. If we don't learn from the past, we are bound to repeat the same behaviors. By marrying and still being a child myself, I had no idea of how to choose a mate. I chose someone with characteristics like my father, though they were more blatant than my father's and even though they were characteristics that I did not like. I saw my mother and father fuss and argue and in their last days together, even fight. I never saw him beat her up. It was always tit for tat. If he hit her, she hit him back.

Eddie and I didn't have fights. He would haul off and hit me and I wouldn't even know he was mad or what had made him mad. I didn't fight back. I never knew how to be ready. I hated fussing and arguing. But I also knew he was wrong and I was afraid of him. One time my grandmother knew he had beaten me because one side of my face was swollen. She told me that I wasn't supposed to just take beatings, that I was supposed to fight back. So I tried it. She said to pick up anything I could find and hit him with it. He hit me and I picked up the broom and conked him over the head. My mistake! He beat me with his fist, knocked me down and I fell over the baby's stroller. I laid there and didn't try to fight back anymore, especially since I was pregnant with Edward. I couldn't believe that someone would beat you up and they knew you were pregnant. I came to realize that even though I thought I loved him, he certainly didn't love me. At least, not the way I understood love. I learned that you can't make anyone else do anything. Even though we were very young, he had his own mind and no one could do anything to change him. He had no desire to change.

We were taught not to be unequally yoked with unbelievers. As kids we knew that meant we should not marry someone who was not a Christian. I felt that I was receiving my just due for being disobedient to this principle. I have since learned that this is a principle that goes beyond being a Christian and non-Christian. Two people cannot walk together or be in fellowship or union unless they agree. Two yoke of oxen had to be the same height and weight to make a team to be able to pull a load. Two people in a relationship should not only be equal spiritually, but in all other areas as well, i.e., in their values, intellectually, in their understanding about life.

My second husband was also an abusive person. He was domineering and insisted on having control over me and the children. When I would question him about anything, he would accuse me of not allowing him to be the man and not wanting to be submissive to him. This was not true. I just didn't always agree with him. I didn't see anything wrong with expressing how I felt about something. After so many tongue lashings and verbal whippings, I remember I became quieter and quieter. I was never to disagree with him in public about anything. I had no problem with that, but he wasn't always right. After our separation, my girlfriend told me that they didn't know I could talk or had an opinion about anything, because I just always sat in the corner and he did all the talking. This is what he insisted on and I was obedient to that.

He was cruel and abusive in his punishment of the kids. The punishment usually exceeded the crime. On this, I couldn't keep quiet. He would whip the kids with a belt across their legs, making welts. They would have to sit there still until he finished whipping and lecturing between hits. One day, when I couldn't' stand it any longer, I told him to stop. He said, "what?" I said, "don't hit him anymore and I mean it." I was ready to tag, if necessary. He stopped. Then he said if I didn't want him to discipline the kids, then I could raise them myself. I said, "whatever, but don't hit him anymore." I think this was Edward. He never could make Ed cry and Edward disliked him greatly for trying to break his spirit. He (Edward) just stayed out of his way.

There was something about me (my spirit) that would not let me just give in all the time. Even though I was afraid, I never would do or put up with any and everything just to have someone in my life. I would rise up when I'd had enough. Too many times, I waited too long before rising up, but I didn't always know what to do.

The one time in my marriage that my second husband hit me for answering him back, I left and came home to Illinois for a week so I could think. Though it had taken him years to do this, I knew he might do it again. When I learned of his molestation of my child, I realized that I and the rest of the family had been abused.

Looking back, all of my relationships have been with men who have been abusive. I know I got involved with such men because of my own low self esteem and lack of knowledge as to how to look for or select a mate. They wanted to have control in some way over me and misused the power that they had. By caring about them and the relationship, I gave up too much of myself, thus giving them too much power. I was afraid of them, afraid of any hurt, whether physical or mental.

I've learned not to give my whole self to anyone except God. Giving one's whole self is too much power to give another human being and it's not fair to them or yourself. I've learned how to keep some of me for me, how to be good to myself and how not to expect someone else to make me feel good about me. If someone else makes me feel good, it's okay, but I don't expect it or have to have it from someone else. I've learned how to fight back when necessary. I expose injustice if I see or feel it. I will not accept abuse of any kind. I believe two people can talk and reason and work out any conflict, but there does not need to be power struggles. We are human beings equally. I need no one in my life who can't respect me as an equal. Our roles in life may not be equal, but we, as humans are equal.

Mankind was put in the position by God to have dominion (control) over all the earth. Men have an innate desire to control. If he has no control in his own life, he tries to control whoever is in his life. Many times he doesn't know or want to know what it means to be in control. Control does not have to be a negative thing. In fact, it is positive, when acted out properly. It means one takes responsibility for what he has been given. That means wife, home, children, church, job, whatever. This taking control of responsibilities always brings about positive results. When positive results do not occur, one should look and see why. Probably, change is needed.

Witnessing abuse in anyone's life is very hurtful to me, because I **know** how it "feels".

9

TO MY CHILDREN

Though this book speaks of my life individually, it is also about you since you have been in my life since your births. I want to encourage you with the following verse from the bible: "Being confident of this, that He who began a good work in you will carry it on to completion until the day of Jesus Christ." Phillipians 1:6

At this time and space, you have overcome many obstacles and been challenged on many fronts. I want you to know that I've seen your struggles and pleaded with God on your behalf at every instance of which I have been aware. I've dedicated this book to you all because of the contribution you've made in enriching my life.

I never dreamed I'd have seven children, but I've been richly blessed by the seven of you to not only be your mother but your friend as well. I am so proud of all of you.

Steven LaMonte
Director, Youth Services & Special Events
Louisville Urban League, Louisville, KY

My firstborn, who was the smallest at birth, but grew to be tall, handsome and steady as a rock. You've been through it all with me. You took the responsibility of being the oldest and the big brother so seriously. You were unselfish and protective in caring for your siblings and for me. Sometimes I could see that it got to be too much for you and you had to back away. I understood. I always felt your care and concern for me. However, I wanted you to have a life of your own, so I tried not to lean on you so much.

I'm sure there were many times in your early life when you were so afraid, but there was no one for you to turn to. I remember when I had to leave you and Cindy in Pittsburgh when we moved back to Illinois. You didn't want to leave then and not graduate with your class. That was so hard for me to do. But I had to trust what I knew was in you.

I was so proud of you when you graduated from Peabody High School. You were able to do what I had not done. You stayed and worked and took care of yourself and completed your goal to finish high school and graduate with your class.

Then you came home to Illinois and made us proud again by becoming a Police Cadet at age nineteen on the Danville Police Force,. You worked at Friendly Town in Lincoln Park instructing school children about safety until you were old enough (21) to join the Police force as a Law Enforcement Officer. I remember when you received the David Farnsworth Scholarship Award to attend Danville Area community college for your Associates Degree in law enforcement. I remember when we came to Springfield for your graduation ceremony and how sharp you looked in your uniform. Although I was always concerned about you as a police officer, and I was also very proud that you wanted to serve humanity in this way. When you had the opportunity to work undercover it caused me even more concern daily before you left Illinois to move to Kentucky. Then you worked law enforcement there also in the city and in the county.

You've always loved working with kids and I always felt that was because you wanted to give some kids what you didn't get, as well as, give them some things you've learned from life. The above are just a few of your accomplishments. You've had many. You continue to choose jobs and professions where you are helping people, and in particular, kids.

There have also been dark days for you. Struggles with depression, alcohol, unsuccessful relationships and failed marriages. We've prayed through and cried through a lot of things. I am thankful that we've been able to talk about almost anything and that you've been able to express your feelings to me even if those feelings hurt me. I know the women in your life have not always understood our closeness, but we've been through a lot together and have drawn strength from one another.

I am so proud of the man you've become. You have never lost your sensitivity to others nor your hope for a brighter future. Thanks for the granddaughter you gave us. Don't worry about the future; remember the Bible verse.

I pray to live and see the many more things God will accomplish in and through you, my firstborn.

Cynthia Delores

Dual Diagnosis Counselor
Community Services Bureau and Merry View Hospital
Norfolk, VA

My first daughter. Much of this book is about you because what happened in your life impacted my life and all of our lives so greatly.

You were a pretty little bubbly girl with a big smile for everyone. You were the only girl for six years. You were always hyper. We found when you were little that you had an iron deficiency. You had shots for this condition. Aunt Louise loved to buy your dresses and clothes because she only had boys. You were smart and very sociable. Since your childhood was snatched away in such an ugly way, you have had so much to overcome. This has been a tremendous challenge where some people in similar circumstances never recover.

The years have been long. Your estrangement of 16 years from us was hard for all of us. Your believing that we didn't love you or want you around was never true. Your anger was understandable. Your rebellion against everything you had been taught was understandable. But; praise God, you couldn't run away from your foundation. It brought you through and it brought you back to us.

In your desire for learning, you were always going to school. Because of your emotional struggles, you could never finish. Something would always cause you to give out. The time finally came, however, when the ghosts of the past no longer had control over you and you burst forth with a new determination to be you and all that you were meant to be. No more victim, no more addictions, no more pity parties. It meant moving away from the city you were in, but you were willing. We too have prayed and cried our way through those dark and stormy years.

I don't know the words to describe the joy and pride I felt as I watched you march across that stage last spring at Old Dominion University in Norfolk, VA to receive your degree in psychology. What an accomplishment for us! I am still filled with pride and joy as I see you emotionally healthy in graduate school working on your master's degree in education and planning your life's work.

I'm so proud that you want to help others in their struggles with mental and emotional wellness.

Edward Lee Jr.

Entrepreneur, Shasher, Inc.
Painting, Wallpaper & Drywall
Jacksonville, IL

Named after your father, my quiet philosopher. Such a deep thinker, wanting to know the whole truth about the matter. You have never been one of the crowd. You've always preferred to be alone with your thoughts. I remember when you didn't want to go to school. Too many kids, I guess. You and Chris were always together and I don't think you liked it when they separated you two at school. You were always so quiet, it was hard to know what you were thinking or feeling. But you had a very strong will. No one could make you do anything you didn't want to. As a baby, you had a ready smile for everyone.

At an early age, it was clear that you wanted to fix things. You were always taking something apart to see how it was made or how it worked. I'll never forget you blowing out the speaker in my good radio or all of the inventions you hooked up in your room.

Though you didn't like school, you did well in your classes, especially if you liked them or the teacher. When you were skipped from the seventh to the eighth grade, it was because they were having vocational classes that you really liked. You liked to work. You liked to make things. You loved to earn your own money. You were always independent. You also had a way with the girls.

Being the strong willed person that you were, we had a few run-ins regarding who was the boss, you or me. It grieved me when you quit school and thought you needed to leave home because you didn't want me telling you what to do. I understood the rebellion but I had to keep the authority because I was responsible for you and knew that I knew what was best for you, especially at the age of sixteen. I really appreciated you telling me after you were grown that I was right in the way I handled you. I appreciate your knowing the challenge you were.

You gave me my first grandchild. I was so upset that you and Terry were having a baby and not married, but when Shalon was born, it was a thrill down to my toes. I understood what all this grandmother fuss was about. I didn't care that I was a young grandmother. I had been a young mother. She was so pretty and perfect and she looked just like Cindy did when she was born. Though I did not plan on babysitting, I did. Many times you all needed someone when you were both working. I was glad when the two of you married and when we were blessed with Sheri as well.

71

You surprised me and made me proud when you decided at the age of nineteen to go into business for yourself. You had worked with a painting contractor when we lived in Pittsburgh, with your uncle in Louisville, and with a weatherization program in Danville, so you had quite a bit of experience. You started out and did well as a painting contractor, bought you a little house, remodeled it and used all the skills you had learned. You could do it all, painting, plumbing, electrical, carpentry. That was over twenty years ago. You are now a successful businessman who had no formal training—just a tremendous gift from God.

You have stuck to what you believed in. You've had many demons and challenges. I'm sure I don't know them all. But I know you have wrestled with the demons of alcohol and drug addictions and gambling. Our talks over the years have been filled with learning and recognition of these struggles. Our talks have also been sweet as we've rejoiced over every victory won. I remember how distressed you were over your father's death in 1984 and how you reached out to your paternal grandparents, aunts and uncles so you could better understand that side of your family and yourself.

In your success you are still always willing to lend a helping hand to anyone in need because you know where your blessings have come from. All of you have allowed God to be the father you did not have and He has never failed any one of us.

Christopher Dean
Ordained Minister
Mental Health Counselor
Champaign, IL

My youngest son. The ambassador (reaching out to everybody). The befriender (always there to be of help), the caretaker, (always taking care of somebody), the family person, (loving "all" of his family), the ordained minister, (dedicated to the mission of being a servant for God and leading others to a relationship with Him).

You too were a friendly, bubbly little boy who always said what he thought. Thank God, you've gained "some" wisdom in that department. Your friendliness and genuine love for people has carried you in so many instances through your years. You've always been active with people, but not necessary in group things except at church.

I remember when you decided to go into the military service. When the man hollered and cussed at you, you left, got back on the bus and came back home, deciding that was not for you if that was the way they had to talk to you. Then you decided to go to Louisville to attend Bible College at our Alma Mater. I never wanted to influence you to go into the ministry. I felt that should be a choice one made for themselves because of all the sacrifice that is involved. And after what had happened in our ministry, I was afraid to try to influence anyone in that area. However, I was pleased when you decided to go. I know you had many unforgettable experiences (good and bad) there. I was disappointed when you quit, but I knew it was because you were not ready yet. You also decided against a professional career in music after starting to head that way.

It was after you had gone away to college that you began to have seizures. After receiving treatment came the realization of your childhood abuse. It was very interesting that at the death of your stepfather's twin brother, you told him about your seizures and he told you that they were psychological and that when you discovered what you were suppressing, they would go away. This was wild since he was a part of the memory you didn't want to acknowledge.

The years that followed this revelation have been like a roller coaster ride. So many times when you were down, I was afraid that you couldn't or wouldn't get up again. Anger, rebellion, depression, addictions, victimizations, bad relationships and a failed marriage followed. A search for your true self which took ten years to complete. This anguish has been so deep.

But all has not been dark. Beyond all of this there have been many positive things and relationships. You have had a professional career in mental health, managerial positions in retail, administrative careers in corporate America and two beautiful children. The grace of God has continued to carry you when you could not stand on your own. Oh, so much learning has taken place. One cannot successfully deal with other people and their issues without learning about and dealing with their own. This, you have done and continue to do so. It seems your life has been such a struggle but I believe it is because you have so much to give. I know that you will receive back what you've given to so many.

I am filled with joy when I hear you teach and preach from the word of God. This is truly a gift of yours. You do it so well (and I know the difference). It goes without saying that I also love to hear you sing. What a pleasure it is for me to have you be the minister of the church we attend. I am proud of the very capable job you do.

These last two years you have been faced with the greatest challenge of all, having been told that you have a terminal illness. You have struggled with anger, fear and guilt. Also the many changes in your body, the pain and the many medication you are on. The inability to work a full time job all of the time. And, of course, the fear of the unknown. How will it happen? When will it happen? Will it happen?

In this last year your daughter has also been diagnosed with kidney and heart problems at the young age of 16 years old. She is on the list for a kidney transplant. Seeing your daughter so sick and being helpless to do anything about it lets you know how I feel about your being so ill. I can only pray.

I want to make sure that we all redeem the time given to us because the days are too precious to waste. This is true even if you're not sick, but its especially true for us now. I remember how everybody came home when they learned you were sick. It's because we love one another and are bound by the family ties between us. You are loved and special to us all.

Don't fear the future—remember the scripture, Phil. 1:6.

Angela
Call Center Supervisor
Convergys Corporation
Jacksonville, NC

The only one of my children without a middle name (your father's idea). You are the image of me, not in looks but in thoughts and actions. Who would have thought that you would turn out to be like me in so many ways. I feel especially proud because it feels like a tribute to me.

I used to call you "angel" because you were such a perfect baby and then a perfect little girl. You were so even tempered. You were a pretty little girl with big eyes and a head full of hair. You didn't cry easily and were very friendly to people. You grew up and was happy until your father left.

Though you've always been even tempered, you've also always had a limit as to how far you could be pushed. You were not afraid of a fight if you were pushed too far.

I remember the first trophy you won in elementary school in a Black History contest. All of you have always striven for excellence in whatever you did. I was always one of the proud parents attending the many school programs you were in.

I remember the years when you were sure you were the ugly ducking and I'd have to assure you that you weren't. You just had not come into your own yet. I instructed you to concentrate on the inside of yourself, not on the outside and just look at you now.

Though my heart was broken when you got pregnant while sill in high school, we were delighted over our first grandson. Jonathon was so cute and possessed your even temper. It was our delight to provide for him the first ten months of his life.

Then the wedding! It was really an event, though we really didn't want to give you away yet. You were a pretty child bride and your sister Anedra was your maid of honor. Remember how your brothers cried when they saw you? They said you were just too young to get married. They were sure handsome attendants in their tuxedos, weren't they? I was so pleased to be able to do this for you; to give you a wedding at our home church and invite all of our friends and family.

A lot has happened since then. You had to leave and move to North Carolina because your husband had joined the military. We kept in touch by mail and sometimes by phone. I traveled to California to see you after Asia was born and Jonny was in Japan. I was so upset that you were all the way out there alone and only nineteen or twenty years old. You tried to assure me that you were okay, but I knew better.

You too have had your share of obstacles and challenges. Your heart was broken when your marriage didn't work out. Needless to say, you were both too young to be equipped to know how to make a relationship work. You stayed and you really tried. I was confident of that.

You came home with your children and immediately found employment to take care of yourself and the children. You were never a burden on us.

Learning how to have successful relationships with men has been as much of a struggle for you as it has for me. Thank God that we have both concluded that this has been out of ignorance on our parts and at this stage in our lives, we're finally getting it together.

I know you have experienced physical and mental abuse in some of your relationships. When you chose to try marriage again, the happiness was short lived. The mental abuse was devastating. The embarrassment that your spouse put you through was humiliating. You again doubted your self worth and had some real struggles with depression and self esteem. We cried and prayed and prayed and cried and became very good friends as you worked your way through your failed marriage.

It was a very interesting development when the children's father began contacting you and made it known that he was interested in the two of you trying again. You both had remarried and gone your separate ways. These marriages had not worked for either of you.

I am pleased to see the two of you together again to finish the job of raising your two children. Jonathon is in his first year of college. .I am proud of the woman you have become, of the leader you are, the

75

professional person you've become and of the great mother you are and that you consider me your best friend.

Anedra Kayleen
Medical Transcriptionist
Carle Clinic
Urbana, IL

My sixth child. So quiet, intellectual, gifted and strong willed.

You were the baby in the house for five years and had no intention of moving over for the one that came after you. You came home from the hospital crying and fretful. You were that way for months. We discovered that you had an upper respiratory infection that would come often. Your temperature would go sky high and we'd have to rush you to the hospital when you could not breathe. You grew out of some of this as you got older.

You too were a cute little bundle of joy with a head full of curls. I used to tease you about being the first kindergarten drop out. You loved pre-school, but you hated kindergarten. I don't know why. You were not fond of elementary nor high school either which I thought was strange because you were so smart. We know that it had nothing to do with your ability to learn, it was the learning environment you didn't like. You didn't like being with all those kids.

You, also are a quiet, deep thinker and a strong willed person. Being strong willed is a good quality that allows one to stick to something until they arrive at their desired goal. You've proven this many times. I know it's hard for you that your children are also strong willed, but you handle it well since you understand it. This is mistaken many times for stubbornness and sometimes it is.

I have been grieved over your pain and the fact that I didn't know you were in pain for a long time. I knew there were some self esteem issues, but I didn't know the root of them. I do remember that you were very upset also when your father left. You were angry at both of us for a long time. I realize when you were in pain and need, I was in the midst of pain and trying to provide for us. I was not available to you and I'll always be sorry for that.

I know that as you grew up, you saw and felt all of the many different struggles and challenges of the older children. You said that you never wanted to cause me grief like the other children. You also said you never wanted to grow up and leave home. We've learned that it is not so easy to control what will happen nor what we'll do and not do. You came to be 18 and out of school and had to make decisions for yourself.

I remember your graduation from high school. I said I was going to give you a big party because that was a hard twelve years. We had a fabulous party and everyone came. You and I were equally glad that these twelve years were over.

I was also pleased when you did finally decide to go to college. You were gorgeous at your graduation and made us all proud when you sang for your class, "There's a winner in you." I knew you were singing about yourself. This was another high day of celebration for us. I know singing is another one of your true gifts and I trust that one day you will get the opportunity to sing professionally and make records since that's your strong desire.

I know that you were so disappointed in yourself when you too got pregnant out of wedlock like me and your sisters. But you were also thrilled to give birth to Arlen who was someone for you to give your love to. You were much older so at least you weren't a teenage mother. I know that part of your reason for leaving and moving so far away was so that you wouldn't be a burden to us. But a mother's love is very close to God's love; you can't get away from it. So when things did not work out with your friend in Virginia, I had to come out there and see about you to encourage you and assure you that things would work out for you. You did get a job shortly after my visit. You got your income tax return and purchased your own car. You were working and taking care of Arlen, had made some friends and were coming into your own. You also started therapy to overcome your fears and depression. I was happy for you.

I am so sorry that part of your adult struggles and challenges have been the same as mine. That you met someone, fell in love and married him, only to then have the traumatic experience of that person you love and trust sexually abuse your child who was only 4 years old. Again, I came out there to see about you. We had been there to visit after the birth of your new baby. Six weeks later I had to come back. I knew you no longer wanted to live or deal with this situation. But you did.

Through much pain and prayer, you are where you are. It has been four years and therapy for you and Arlen, but there's light at the end of this tunnel. One only has to hear you sing. You and God know what he's brought you through and it comes out in your singing. I can't hear you sing about God's goodness without my heart leaping in my chest and tears filling my eyes.

You are a responsible parent and a loving mother and a loyal and good friend to those with whom you have become friends.

77

I've watched you grow and gain confidence with each accomplishment. I am so excited about what the future holds for you!

Alicia Louise
Certified Nurse's Assistant
Urbana, IL

Number seven, the baby, named after your Aunt Louise. We knew you would be the last baby born to either of us so it was a pleasure to give you her name for your middle name.

You have benefited from all who have gone before you. You have also suffered some by being at the end. This is because by the time your turmoil started, I was so tired. I didn't give you any less, but I was tired.

I called you my angel, also, because I feel you saved my life. When I found out about your father's indiscretions, I was seven months pregnant with you. I had no desire to live, so I wouldn't eat, I felt I couldn't. The doctor instructed me that I had to eat and take care of myself for your well being. So, I did. When you were born I was so happy that you were all right. You, too were a pretty little baby with a head full of curls. You and Anedra looked just alike. You were a happy baby.

Your father and I were still together when you were born. You were two years old when he left. You cried all the time after he left. One time he came to see you all and when he left you screamed for him to come back. He said he couldn't come back to visit because he couldn't stand to see you all upset like that. So he never came again. I'm sure that you have carried that first feeling of abandonment within you.

But all was not dark because you were our baby. Everyone saw to your needs and desires. Mother talked about how before you could get a cry out, someone was there seeing what you wanted.

We were back home in Illinois when you started head Start. This was a very good experience for you and you stopped being so whiney. Your graduation from head start was so cute. Me and your Aunt Louise were there. You were a pleasant, loving and sensitive child. You were active in school and in all sorts of activities.

Remember when you were Santa Claus at one of your school's Christmas programs? We really got a laugh out of you being a black Santa Claus among so many white children, but no one seemed to mind.

Then you blossomed as a track star. We sure attended a lot of track meets over the years, locally and at state finals until you decided you didn't want to run anymore. You always reminded me of a gazelle. Your stride was so long and graceful. You, like your brother Chris always brought a friend along, so it was never just you. Cindy was that way too.

By high school you were not running anymore but you were involved in the school's show choir. Though normally for juniors and seniors, you auditioned as a sophomore and got selected. You were cute, personable and shapely. The boys were plentiful, to my dismay. You also had a beautiful voice (and still do) so you were a lead singer right away. You reminded me so much of myself at your age. I was definitely afraid for you. Your first real boyfriend was a fatal attraction that lasted almost 2 years. That left a bad taste in all of our mouths since I had to have your brothers involved for your protection.

I remember sitting at one of your performances when you sang a duet with one of the male lead singers. It was so pretty, I just cried. I also felt like you would not have the chances that you deserved to have. I don't know why I felt that way, but I did. Maybe because I felt I had so little control over you.

When we found out that you were pregnant in your junior year of high school, even though I was devastated, I knew what this did to you. You were so disappointed in yourself that you lost your sense of self worth. I've watched you punish yourself over the years but I'm thankful now that you are working to overcome that negative behavior. Your entering into an abusive relationship was the result of your not caring enough about yourself as well as not knowing how to select a partner and you were too young for a serious relationship.

You gave up your schooling, having entered your first year in college. You decided to seek training to be a CNA (Certified Nurses Assistant) since it was short term and you could stick it out that long. We were there for your graduation, of course. You too sang for your class. We were very proud as you sang "The Greatest Love of All."

I have seen you fight hard against the challenges that you have faced. I was so proud of you when you put yourself in the hospital to overcome your addiction to drugs. And when you could attest that you already knew who the "higher power" was that they talk about. Also, when you began to forgive yourself for turning your back on everything you had been taught. When you married and also accepted your husband's daughter to raise who was one year older than Steven.

Your struggle and challenge in recent years has been the greatest of all. Having your husband stricken with encephalitis when you were in your eighth month of pregnancy with his and your baby. Having him go into a coma for over three months and suffer some brain damage as a result. Praying constantly for his recovery, then having him awaken and not know you, at first. You demonstrated nothing but loving patience as you traveled daily to Springfield to be at his bedside and took care of your home and children. Then when he came out of the coma, nursed him back to partial health, only to have him leave you and go live with his family was a tremendous blow. I know you asked the questions why and when would the hurt end. Now he has returned and you must deal with the many issues that face him since his life is totally different and he is disabled. His brain damage means he will have seizures for the rest of his life without the medications.

I know that God is carrying you through right now just as He has the rest of us as the two of you are separated and in the process of obtaining a divorce. .

I am very proud of you and the woman and mother you are. I eagerly anticipate the good things that are yet in store for you.

I believe we are a special family. That we've been allowed special challenges to not only shape and mold us, but also to empower others. I have always told all of you that you are special (not in a conceited way) and I know that it is true because no matter what we have gone through, we all still care about others. We are not bitter. We have a great sense of humor. No one can laugh at us like we can laugh at ourselves. But most of all, all of us can attest to what prayer and faith in God can do.

THINGS TO REMEMBER

- ✓ You can't fix what's broken in someone else.
- ✓ You can't change anyone except yourself.
- ✓ If a person isn't all you want them to be, do not enter a relationship with them. Be strong enough to walk away before you make a commitment of a permanent nature. It is better be disappointed early than after you have invested a lot of time and emotion.
- ✓ If you are in financial trouble, stop buying. Don't live beyond your means. Look at your finances weekly. If you have more going out than you have coming in, get another job. Figure out how to cut your expenses until they match your income.
- ✓ Don't be afraid to take risks if you've considered everything and counted the costs.
- ✓ If you're stressed about something, handle it right away. Don't let stress pile up on you. If you can fix it, do so. If not, accept it and let it go.
- ✓ If you truly have a desire to be made whole (well), all of the pieces that are required to put you together again (like Humpty Dumpty) will be put into place in your lifetime.

✓ Don't get hung up on the notion of love or disillusioned by broken relationships. Love is not magic, it only 'feels" like it, especially when it is real. Love is good and is from God because God is love. Love is patient, kind, does not envy, does not boast, is not proud, is not rude, always trusts, always hopes, never fails.

✓ Take the time necessary to weigh decisions. Errors in judgement are yours and the consequences from these errors will be yours.

✓ Truth is revealed—seek it.

✓ We are the tools God uses to manifest His work here on earth. When a builder builds a house, he gets the praise and glory, not the tools that were used. We should learn not to seek honor for ourselves, at least not the honor that belongs to the power Source. We can do nothing without Him. We are nothing without Him. We are not the power—only the tools. IT'S NOT ABOUT YOU.

ADDENDUM

I've learned—

- That you cannot make someone love you. All you can do is be someone who can be loved. The rest is up to them.
- That no matter how much I care, some people just don't care back.
- That it takes years to build up trust, and only seconds to destroy it.
- That it's not what you have in your life, but who you have in your life that counts.
- That you can get by on charm for 15 minutes, after that, you'd better know something.
- That you shouldn't compare yourself to the best others can do.
- That you can do something in an instant that can give you heartache for life.
- That it's taken me a long time to become the person I want to be.
- That you should always leave loved ones with kind words every time you see them.
- That you can keep going long after you think you can't.
- That we are responsible for what we do, no matter how we feel.
- That either you control your attitude or it controls you.
- That regardless of how hot and steamy a relationship is at first, the passion fades and there had better be something there to replace it.
- That heroes are the people who do what has to be done when it needs to be done, regardless of the consequences.
- That money is a lousy way of keeping score.
- That my best friend and I can do anything or nothing and have the best time.
- That sometimes the people you expect to kick you when you're down will be the ones to help you get back up.

- That sometimes when I'm angry I have the right to be angry, but that doesn't give me the right to be cruel.
- That true friendship continues to grow, even over the longest distance. The same goes for true love.
- That just because someone doesn't love you the way you want them to doesn't mean they don't love you with all they have.
- That maturity has more to do with what types of experiences you've had and what you've learned from them and less to do with how many birthdays you've celebrated.
- That you should never tell a child their dreams are unlikely or outlandish. Few things are more humiliating, and what a tragedy it would be if they believed it.
- That your family won't always be there for you. It may seem funny, but people who aren't related to you can take care of you and love you and teach you to trust people again. Families aren't always biological.
- That no matter how good a friend is, they're going to hurt you once in a while and you must forgive them for that.
- That it isn't always enough to be forgiven by others. Many times the hardest one to forgive is yourself.
- That no matter how bad your heart is broken, the world doesn't stop for grief.
- That our background and circumstances may have influenced who we are, but we are responsible for who we become.
- That, just because two people argue, it doesn't mean they don't love each other and just because they don't argue, doesn't mean they do.
- That we don't have to change friends if we understand that friends change.
- That you shouldn't be so eager to find out a secret. It could change your life forever.
- That two people can look at the exact same thing and see something totally different.
- That no matter how you try to protect your children, they will eventually get hurt and you will hurt in the process.
- That your life can be changed in a matter of hours by people who don't even know you.

- ◆ That even when you think you have no more to give, when a friend cries out to you, you will find the strength to help.
- ◆ That credentials on the wall do not make you a decent human being.
- ◆ That the people you care about most in life are taken from you too soon.
- ◆ That it's hard to determine where to draw the line between being nice and not hurting people's feelings and standing up for what you believe.

-Unknown

THE END

The Author Says......

One cannot write a book about their own life without feeling very exposed.

In what I perceive my life to be, that is, one of service to others, I have found writing this book to be the next step for me. Nothing else reaches the masses like the written word.

*Everyone has a story. While each story is different, each story is the same. Our stories are all of difficulties and defeats, struggles and triumphs, battles and victories, sorrow and pain. Our lives hold secrets we'd rather keep, skeletons we'd rather not let out. However, in telling our own particular story, **SOMEONE** else recognizes him or herself or at least recognizes their particular struggle or issues. **SOMEONE** can be encouraged and motivated to overcome. **SOMEONE** can know it's all right to expose themselves in this way. Those who love you will love you still. Those who condemn you were not true friends or they lack understanding of what you have done and why.*

While we are all different, we are all also the same, with the same needs and desires for love and acceptance. Love from our God, the Creator and love from one another.

As you read this book, may you understand that what ever happens to you in this life, is for your learning. You must take the lessons and allow them to empower you to overcome the challenges that you face. When you are victorious, it gives others hope.

Susie Mitchell Doswell

Susie & Louise, 5 yrs & 7 yrs old

Susie, 7 yrs old

Junior Club at Mrs. Clark's

At Church

Susie & Friends (1955) Sister, Louise, far left back row

In the Choir (front middle)

In the Choir (far left, next to Mother)

Susie 14 yrs old

Home in Pittsburgh, 7604 Bennett St.

Graduation (1964) Thurman & Susie

Edward L. Matchem Sr. (deceased - 1984)

Wilson & Susie at marriage reception

Wilson & Susie (1993)

Sister Louise, Father, Mother, Susie (1991 - 50 yrs old)

7 children - back row: Steven, Christopher, Edward front row: Alicia, Cynthia, Anedra, Angela

Entire Family at 50th birthday celebration

Susie Mitchell Doswell

ABOUT THE AUTHOR

SUSIE MITCHELL DOSWELL is the Director of the Annual Christian Womens Retreat which is an organization of over 200 women and girls who meet each year in a different city in the United States. The organization is 23 years old and is for the purpose of spiritual, mental, emotional and physical growth through learning. The participants come from allover the United States, as well as, the Grand Cayman Islands. Mrs. Doswell has been the Coordinator/Director for 18 years.

She is a wife and mother of seven children. She is an alumnus of the College of the Scriptures in Louisville, Kentucky. She is a speaker, teacher and counselor to many. She is a capable organizer and encourager. She serves her church as Choir Director and Christian Education Director to name a few things that she is responsible for. She is qualified to address the issues of: pre-marital sex, teen pregnancy, incest, addictions, divorce, remarriage, relationships, abuse, spiritual life in the church and many more.

Mrs. Doswell decided to make her first book autobiographical as a tool for hope and encouragement. That no matter if one falls down, that they know they too can get back up and go on to victories as she has done.

www.ingramcontent.com/pod-product-compliance
Lightning Source LLC
Chambersburg PA
CBHW051448280526
45785CB00003B/1483